Legal Theory Today
Law as a Social Institution

Legal Theory Today

General Editor of the Series

Dr John Gardner, Reader in Legal Theory, King's College, London

Forthcoming titles:

Law after Modernity by Sionaidh Douglas-Scott
Law and Ethics by John Tasioulas
Risks and Legal Theory by Jenny Steele
Law and Aesthetics by Adam Gearey
Evaluation and Legal Theory by Julie Dickson

Law as a Social Institution

Hamish Ross

·H A R T·
PUBLISHING

OXFORD – PORTLAND OREGON
2001

Hart Publishing
Oxford and Portland, Oregon

Published in North America (US and Canada) by
Hart Publishing c/o
International Specialized Book Services
5804 NE Hassalo Street
Portland, Oregon
97213-3644
USA

Distributed in the Netherlands, Belgium and Luxembourg
by
Intersentia, Churchillaan 108
B2900 Schoten
Antwerpen
Belgium

Hart Publishing is a specialist legal publisher based in Oxford,
England.
To order further copies of this book or to request a list of other
publications please write to:

Hart Publishing, Salter's Boatyard, Folly Bridge,
Abingdon Road, Oxford OX1 4LB
Telephone: +44 (0)1865 245533 or Fax: +44 (0)1865 794882
e-mail: mail@hartpub.co.uk
WEBSITE: http//www.hartpub.co.uk

British Library Cataloguing in Publication Data
Data Available
ISBN 1–84113–230–6 (hardback)
1–84113–231–4 (paperback)

Typeset by Hope Services (Abingdon) Ltd.
Printed and bound in Great Britain on acid-free paper
by
Biddles Ltd, www.biddles.co.uk

For Sam and Nicky

General Editor's Preface

Hamish Ross's important book is the second in the *Legal Theory Today* series, and like the first (*Law in its own Right* by Henrik Palmer Olsen and Stuart Toddington) it keeps faith with the idea that originally animated the series. It sets out to build a bridge between ways of thinking about law that are commonly thought to be worlds apart. In the case of *Law as a Social Institution*, the bridge is between "analytical" and "sociological" jurisprudence.

Ross takes seriously H L A Hart's remark in the preface to *The Concept of Law* (1961) that the work can be read either as a work of "analytical jurisprudence" or as a work of "descriptive sociology". What exactly, wonders Ross, would be the difference between these two readings? The answer is fascinating. It turns out that the common contrast between "analytical" and "sociological" jurisprudence is a false contrast, for a successful sociological jurisprudence needs to be no less analytical—no less concerned with the dissection and classification of concepts—than any other. What marks it out and commends it as a specifically sociological jurisprudence (says Ross) is firstly its distinctive focus on legal norms as social norms, and secondly its studying of its subject matter from a distinctive perspective, namely the "hermeneutic" perspective of the detached insider.

Not all legal theory shares or needs to share these particular foci. After all, many legal norms are not social norms and so cannot be studied as social norms. And at least some theoretical problems faced by lawyers demand investigation from a committed—true believer's—perspective. Nor does Ross deny these points. What he argues, however, is that there remains logical space for a distinctively sociological jurisprudence, and that Hart's *The Concept of Law* should be regarded as a serious, but flawed, attempt to produce one.

What struck me most about this book on first encounter was the total absence from its pages of the kind of verificationist scepticism about the domain of the *rational* that so damages many attempts to think sociologically about law, or to locate law among the social sciences. Like Weber but unlike many self-styled Weberians, Ross is no reductionist about human agency and harbours no subliminal longing to convert rules or standards (or the institutions ordered by them) into mere causal or probabilistic generalisations. That is why there are moments when his criticisms of Hart resonate with those of another bridge-builder in jurisprudence, namely John Finnis. One might think that no body of work in the philosophy of law could be further removed from the "sociological" and more immersed in the "metaphysical" than Finnis's. But there we have another false contrast. It is no accident that Finnis, like Ross, is so immersed in Weber's work. Sociology too must have its metaphyics, its irreducible presuppositions. In this book Hamish Ross formally re-opens the metaphysics of legal sociology to scrutiny. In the process he carries forward, while at the same time reorienting in a direction markedly different from Finnis's, the double-sided enterprise announced by Hart in the preface of *The Concept of Law*. I hope you enjoy the result as much as I did.

John Gardner
University College, Oxford
19 March 2001

Preface and Acknowledgements

Following its publication in 1961 and during the closing decades of the twentieth century one of the most celebrated texts in the literature of jurisprudence was the subject of unremitting academic attention, speculation and debate in the English-speaking world. In a variety of ways *The Concept of Law* redrew the boundaries of jurisprudence and its sub-disciplines: philosophy of law, legal science, legal theory, analytical jurisprudence and sociology of law. Its author, H L A Hart, came to be ranked among the leading jurists of the century and established a "following", many of whose most influential adherents have themselves made highly important contributions to the literature of jurisprudence over the last four decades. During the 1920s *Economy and Society* was published in Germany. It was a monument of scholarship, staggering in its scope, complexity and depth of insight. Since publication its authority has remained virtually unchallenged. Max Weber's encyclopaedic masterpiece, along with other important writings such as *The Protestant Ethic and the Spirit of Capitalism*, unquestionably established Weber's reputation as the greatest, if not the least controversial, social theorist of the modern age.

In this short book I have tried to identify a few common strands of thought running through both Weber and Hart. I tentatively point to ways in which—if Hart (say) had been more Weberian—the explanatory power of *The Concept of Law* might have been enhanced. What is interesting overall, perhaps, is that Hart emerges relatively unscathed from quite recent accusations of "sociological isolationism". Moreover, despite a measure of sometimes hostile scepticism surrounding Hart's claim that *The Concept of Law* was "an essay in descriptive sociology" it has become clear to me in the light of the writings of Weber and Neil MacCormick that the book may, perhaps, be better described as an inchoate essay in *interpretive* sociology, and a quite creditable one at that.

If I am not mistaken, what I believe *The Concept of Law* does in various places—though often not especially clearly—is sow the seeds of a potentially more thoroughgoing sociological approach to legal theory. I have attempted merely to outline the skeleton of such an approach in chapters 5, 6 and 7, using as a springboard a critique of aspects of the analytical *core* of *The Concept of Law* which I refer to as Hart's "nucleic expository theory". At appropriate points this outline theoretical approach draws on writers as diverse as Talcott Parsons and W N Hohfeld. A major thesis of this book—in fact, one of its most significant conclusions—is that Hohfeld's eight-term relational configuration of "jural relations" mirrors, in a legal institutional context, the relationality of human social behaviour in general. In other words, relationality is so deeply embedded in the subjective meaning of human social action that, I argue, we cannot lightly ignore the manifestations of this in the institutional and conceptual apparatuses of the law.

Part of this book started life as a doctoral thesis submitted at Glasgow University in 1989. The thesis, entitled *A Sociological Analysis of the Jural Relation*, dwells more searchingly on Hohfeld's analysis than I have been able to do within the scope of this book. Most of the assistance that I wish to acknowledge here relates to the writing-up period of the thesis during the late 1980s. I acknowledge the patient and friendly critical advice given to me by Michael Lessnoff of the Department of Politics, Glasgow University. Thanks are also due to Tom Campbell, Elspeth Attwooll and Gerry Maher, then of the Department of Jurisprudence at Glasgow. I also acknowledge more recent comments offered by David Goldberg. While writing up this book during 1999–2000 I benefited from the enlightened research policy fostered by Professor Rebecca Wallace at Napier University School of Law.

My most sincere appreciation and thanks are due to Neil MacCormick whose inaugural lecture, "Law as Institutional Fact", was an early inspiration for my thesis. Neil first took an interest in my work at the end of 1987. Since then I have benefited immeasurably from his encouraging, constructive criticism. Neil also secured grant funding from the Lindsay Bequest at Edinburgh University in 1992 to enable me to commence writing an earlier version of this book during a short sabbatical from my work as a solicitor. My thanks again, Neil: mentor *et magister*!

I owe a final debt of gratitude to John Gardner for being a most enthusiastic and helpful editor of the series.

Contents

Contents

Note on Abbreviations

CL H L A Hart, *The Concept of Law* (Clarendon Press, Oxford, 2nd ed. 1994), with Postscript edited by Penelope A Bulloch and Joseph Raz.

ES Max Weber, *Economy and Society. An Outline of Interpretive Sociology* (Bedminster Press Inc., New York, 1968), Guenther Roth, Claus Wittich *et al* (eds.). (Translation from German of Max Weber, *Wirtschaft und Gesellschaft. Grundriss der verstehenden Soziologie.*)

LES Max Weber, *Max Weber on Law in Economy and Society* (Harvard University Press, Cambridge, Mass., 1954), with Introduction and annotations by Max Rheinstein. (Translation of chapter VII of 1925 edition of Max Weber, *Wirtschaft und Gesellschaft*: otherwise *Rechtssoziologie* or *Sociology of Law.*)

OSS Max Weber, " 'Objectivity' in Social Science and Social Policy", in Max Weber, *The Methodology of the Social Sciences* (The Free Press, New York, 1949), chapter II. (Translation of Max Weber, "Die 'Objektivität' sozialwis-senschaft-licher und sozialpolitischer Erkenntnis", origi-nally published in *Archiv für Sozialwissenschaft und Sozialpolitik*, 1904.)

PTL Hans Kelsen, *Introduction to the Problems of Legal Theory* (Clarendon Press, Oxford, 1992), with Introduction by Stanley L Paulson. (Translation of the First Edition of Hans Kelsen, *Reine Rechtslehre. Einleitung in die rechtswis-senschaftliche Problematik* (*Pure Theory of Law*, 1934.)

TSEO Max Weber, *The Theory of Social and Economic Organiza-tion* (The Free Press, New York, 1947) revised and edited with Introduction by Talcott Parsons. (Translation from German of Part I of Max Weber, *Wirtschaft und Gesellschaft.*)

1
An Opportunity to Reflect

"The habit of thinking in terms of decades and centuries induces a self-fulfilling delusion and the way people behave—or, at least, perceive their behaviour—really does tend to change accordingly. Decades and centuries are like the clock-cases inside which the pendulum of history swings. Strictly speaking, a new millennium begins every day and every moment of every day. . . ." *Felipe Fernández-Armesto*[1]

An opportunity to reflect

Law is the pendulum of human society, regulating its action and mechanisms. Just as a pendulum sometimes runs behind or ahead of time, so law occasionally leads or lags behind prevailing climates of opinion. When its pendulum breaks down completely a clock becomes functionally useless. Societies similarly suffer from dysfunctional systems of laws. When such a system is no longer in harmony with the communities that it governs, or is insensitive to the interests of minority groups, it may render justice ineptly and inefficiently. In the worst scenario law may give refuge and expression to the darkest, and most malign, forces in the human character. At the third millennium of the Christian world a most remarkable century came to a close: it is timely, at the end of a century which at the same time marked the end of a millennium, to reflect upon the past. The twentieth century was the greatest period of upheaval and change in recorded history. The first half of the century was dominated by two world wars of incomparable ferocity and destructiveness. The final fifty years were characterised by the ideological and military stalemate of the Cold War and by a technological

[1] Felipe Fernández-Armesto, *Millennium* (Black Swan, London, 1996), xiv.

revolution of probably greater significance than the Industrial Revolution of the nineteenth century. These and other momentous events radically refashioned ideas and brought about social, economic, cultural, political and demographic change on a scale that was scarcely conceivable to any previous age. The twentieth century was correspondingly a period of transformation for modes of organising human societies and ordering international relations by legal, political and administrative institutional structures.

The theoretical advancement of the branch of jurisprudence known as legal positivism mirrored some of those changes. Without doubt legal positivism played an important part in the historical progress of ideas in the twentieth century, contributing to a deeper conceptual and philosophical understanding of law.[2] In any scientific discipline—even in the natural sciences—theory may be a product of its historical context. Theoretical models formulated to explain phenomena usually engage with or respond to the specific problems of a given historical era. Those models may be peculiarly adapted to an explanation of phenomena. Inevitably, theory also makes use of insights from earlier times. It may be grafted onto, or represent an advance in, existing knowledge or theoretical approaches. To that extent it may not be anything *other* than a product of its age. Thomas Kuhn has pointed to a historiographic revolution in the study of science characterised by a trend towards identifying new developmental lines for the sciences. Instead of seeking the contributions of science of earlier ages to present scientific knowledge, a

---

[2] A relatively settled commencement point for legal positivists is an insistence on the possibility of analytically separating law "as it is" from law "as it ought to be". Legal philosophers, of course, differ widely in their interpretation of, approach to, and the emphasis to be placed on the consequences of, this starting position. A further important tenet is that law in this sense is seen to be "posited" or created by human act of will as distinct from natural law which can be said to have a divine or metaphysical origin. See H L A Hart, *The Concept of Law* (Clarendon Press, Oxford, 2nd ed. 1994) (*CL*), 302. See also John Finnis on the historical origins and development of the expression "positivism" used in reference to law in "The Truth in Legal Positivism", ch. 7 in Robert P George (ed.) *The Autonomy of Law: Essays on Legal Positivism* (Clarendon Press, Oxford, 1996), 195 *et seq.*

growing number of historians of science have examined the integrity of scientific discoveries relative to their own time.[3] For example, they might ask about the relationship of Galileo's views to those of his teachers, contemporaries and immediate successors in order to give Galileo's discoveries maximum internal coherence and closest fit to nature *as it was then understood*. When examined in their historical context, the major twentieth century writings in the legal positivist tradition appear, on the face of it, and in different ways, to be embedded in the philosophical and scientific milieux of the time. In 1961 one of the foremost jurists of the age, the English legal philosopher H L A Hart (1907–1992), published *The Concept of Law*:[4] a theory of exceptional explanatory power and depth. Hart continued to publish throughout his long career and in some cases, in the light of informed, constructive criticism, clarified or modified positions which he had adopted in his earlier work. Hart established what, in hindsight, could be regarded as a school or "paradigm" of legal thinking which has outlived him.[5] The secondary literature on Hart is, without exaggeration, immense.[6] There are disciplinary or theoretical "offshoots" from—or in some sense traceable back to—his theory, and entirely new theories in some sense "inspired" by his work: for instance the institutional theory of Neil MacCormick. There are also "opposed" or original ways of thinking about law characterised by, among others, the work of the Anglo-American jurist Ronald Dworkin and the (quite separate) critical legal studies movement. The distinct jurisprudential paradigm or model of law formulated by Hart has developed in the light of critical examination, gaining

[3] See Thomas S Kuhn, *The Structure of Scientific Revolutions* (University of Chicago Press, Chicago and London, 3rd ed. 1996), 3.

[4] Above at n. 2.

[5] Ibid., 175 *et seq.* Here Kuhn usefully discusses a variety of senses of the notion of "paradigm".

[6] A list of Hart's main works and biographical information on Hart is given in Neil MacCormick, *H.L.A. Hart* (Edward Arnold (Publishers) Ltd., London, 1981), ch. 1. A more comprehensive list of works by Hart is to be found in Michael D Bayles, *Hart's Legal Philosophy:An Examination* (Kluwer, The Netherlands, 1992). An extensive citation of primary and secondary literature is given at 294–312.

acceptance and "currency" in relevant academic communities. Hart's work continues to inform contemporary debates concerning, among other things, the nature of law and the possibility and aims of a science of law.

Since the late 1960s, however, the Hartian model of legal positivism has been the subject of sustained critical attention and attack. Dworkin, for instance, has been one of the most persistent and illuminating critics of important aspects of Hart's theory.[7] More recently, a body of opinion has questioned whether leading proponents of legal positivism devised modes of explanation that *were* satisfactorily adapted to the main intellectual currents of twentieth century thinking. Disciplines such as sociology and psychology flourished during the century, yet were considered "foreign" to the science of law by another illustrious legal philosopher, the Austrian jurist Hans Kelsen. Those relatively new sciences revealed hitherto unknown problems, issues and challenges in their quest to shed light on the seemingly limitless complexity of human behaviour and human society. The jurist Eugen Ehrlich believed that since law is a social phenomenon, every kind of legal science is a social science in the sense of being part of the theoretical science of society: of sociology.[8] Despite a measure of acceptance that law is a social phenomenon, however, social scientific disciplines were not accorded a central place in Hart's jurisprudence. It seems unsurprising how far legal positivism, as represented in one of its most influential twentieth century texts, *The Concept of Law*, and in voluminous secondary literature, maintained intellectual disengagement with social theory throughout the twentieth century. Two dominant trends in Anglo-American jurisprudential thought—the sociological movement in law[9] and positivist analytical jurisprudence—developed in almost complete isolation from one another, while at the same time the analytical tradition devel-

---

[7] See, for example, Ronald Dworkin, *Taking Rights Seriously* (Fifth Impression) (Gerald Duckworth & Co. Ltd., 1977), especially ch. 2 at 14 *et seq.*

[8] See Eugen Ehrlich, *Fundamental Principles of the Sociology of Law* (Harvard University Press, Cambridge, Mass., 1936), 25.

[9] See, generally, the book of that name by Alan Hunt: *The Sociological Movement in Law* (The MacMillan Press Limited, 1978).

oped separately from②classical and contemporary social theory. At first sight this divergence of trends in legal and social science—which Kelsen's work positively reinforced and Hart's work scarcely impeded—can be seen as a paradox in the historical development of twentieth century legal theory.

On one hand it is clear that Kelsen did not share Ehrlich's belief that legal science and the science of society are part of the same enterprise. Kelsen's explicit opposition to interdisciplinary jurisprudence—"syncretism", as he termed it—reinforced his distinctive approach to law as an autonomous discipline and made Kelsenian legal science seemingly invulnerable to the otherwise pervasive influence of social theory during the twentieth century.[10] Yet Kelsen's legacy is difficult to assess because there is at least a resonance of Max Weber's approach to social theory in Kelsen's distinctive notion of legal meaning (*rechtliche Bedeutung*). Other aspects of Kelsen's work belie the notion that the *Pure Theory of Law*[11] genuinely attained the "purity"—or freedom from the influence of alien disciplines—that Kelsen claimed for it. On the other hand an assessment of Hart's work is attended with difficulty not because of any avowed opposition on his part to the influence of disciplines perceived to be alien, but because of his apparent ambivalence towards such disciplines.[12] Although Hart described his major text, *The Concept of Law*, as an "essay in descriptive sociology" his work in general eschewed mainstream social theory and avoided serious critical—or, indeed, *any*—examination of important social theorists such as Max Weber. Yet while Hart contributed little to the possibility of integrating his theory of law with the theories of leading social theorists his implicit advocacy of a Weberian *Verstehende* or hermeneutic methodology was revealing. For instance, in his notion of the "internal aspect" of rules and in certain other respects Hart inclined markedly towards ideas that had been developed in Weber's social theory and were latterly taken up by sub-disciplines of legal theory such as legal semiotics and legal

[10] See Hans Kelsen, *Introduction to the Problems of Legal Theory* (Clarendon Press, Oxford, 1992) (*PTL*), xxi, xxii (Stanley Paulson's comments at n. 14).

[11] Ibid.

[12] See Hart's observation reproduced at the commencement of ch. 4 below.

hermeneutics. Hart initiated many fertile enquiries, and alluded to analytical tasks, lying squarely in the realm of social theory. Arguably though—as indeed I propose to show in chapter 4 below—Hart often failed to pursue those enquiries and tasks far enough. It is possible that had he done so, he might—for sociologists, at least—have significantly enhanced the explanatory power of his original theory.

In a mature assessment of the significance of Hart's career in the light of two centuries of Anglo-American academic law, William Twining, in 1979, highlighted points of criticism that could be said to exemplify the main themes of a debate that centred around that time on Hart's "sociological isolationism".[13] Twining observed that the distinctive genre of legal philosophy which he termed "Oxonian" (that of Hart and his followers) was at the time of writing "proceeding in almost complete isolation from contemporary social theory and from work in socio-legal studies, with little overt concern with the law in action". But this was only a preliminary assessment based on Twining's reading of a *festschrift* published in 1977 celebrating Hart's then seventieth birthday: *Law, Morality, and Society*.[14] For, in the course of other criticisms, Twining expressed dissatisfaction at what he perceived as the narrowness of the Oxonian philosophical approach. He was thus sceptical of the claim made by the editors of *Law, Morality, and Society* that Hart had integrated twentieth century legal philosophy into "the mainstream of *general* philosophical thought". A more modest claimant might have

[13] See William Twining, "Academic Law and Legal Philosophy: The Significance of Herbert Hart" (1979) 95 *Law Quarterly Review* 557. In what sense has there been a "debate" concerning Hart's sociological isolationism? Apart from Twining's essay, a number of articles are relevant here. See, for example, C M Campbell and Paul Wiles, "The Study of Law in Society in Britain", (1976) 10 *Law and Society Review* 547, esp. 568–74; Brendan Edgeworth, "Legal Positivism and the Philosophy of Language: A Critique of H.L.A. Hart's 'Descriptive Sociology'" (1986) 6 *Legal Studies* 115. See also Peter Goodrich, "The Antinomies of Legal Theory: An Introductory Survey." (1983) 3 *Legal Studies* 1. In Hart's defence there is Martin Krygier "*The Concept of Law* and Social Theory" (1982) 2 *Oxford Journal of Legal Studies* 155.

[14] P M S. Hacker and J Raz (eds) *Law, Morality, and Society: Essays in Honour of H.L.A. Hart* (Clarendon Press, Oxford, 1977).

acknowledged Hart's achievement in integrating legal philosophy into the mainstream of contemporary *British* analytical philosophy but this, as Twining pointed out, was by no means a universally accepted philosophical approach. Twining also pointed to the claim that *The Concept of Law* is an essay in "descriptive sociology". That claim has been disputed elsewhere, although its significance and relevance to Hart's approach have perhaps been exaggerated by commentators, sympathetic and unsympathetic alike.[15] For Twining and others it was scarcely acceptable to describe *The Concept of Law* in those terms when Hart's theoretical *oeuvre* owed more to British linguistic philosophy than to such leading figures in the world of sociology as Weber, Marx, Durkheim, Parsons or Merton. Treating *Law, Morality, and Society* as typifying the Oxonian approach to jurisprudence, Twining was concerned that he was unable to find any reference in the book to these or other major social theorists, let alone a single sustained discussion of their work. Why, in any event—asked Twining—should this type of "sociology" be considered to be *descriptive* rather than interpretive or explanatory?[16]

Twining was not alone in his perception of Hart's apparent neglect of classical and mainstream social theory. A decade later Roger Cotterell pointed out that Hart speculatively philosophises about widely held attitudes to different categories of rules without undertaking an empirical study of actual social conditions.[17] Cotterell argued that Hart's jurisprudence thus defied classification as sociology. Donald Galloway had expressed a similar criticism in 1978, asserting that Hart expends little effort

[15] For example, Krygier, above at n. 13, comments on this claim at 156. Twining, above at n. 13, comments at 566. Roger Cotterell, in *The Politics of Jurisprudence: A Critical Introduction to Legal Philosophy* (Butterworths, London and Edinburgh, 1989) comments at 91 and 95–6. Stephen Guest comments on Hart's claim in his essay, entitled "Two Strands in Hart's Theory of Law: A Comment on the *Postscript* to Hart's *The Concept of Law*", in Stephen Guest (ed.) *Positivism Today* (Dartmouth Publishing, Aldershot, 1996), 30.

[16] As Twining, above at n. 13, at 566–7, remarks: "[I]f law is to be viewed as a social phenomenon, it would seem to be worthwhile at least to explore the relationship between legal theory and social theory, in particular possible connections between theories of law and theories of society".

[17] Cotterrell, above at n. 15, at 95.

in charting the position of law in its social context, offering instead a mere *lawyer's* interpretation of the social phenomenon of law. As a participant in the legal milieu the lawyer was, as it were, trapped on the inside, inescapably committed to institutional ideals and assumptions and unlikely to subject these to critical evaluation. Far from offering an essay in descriptive sociology, Hart proposed "a liberalist's armchair Weltanschauung".[18] In much the same way as Hart's avowedly surgical technique had saved jurisprudence from Austin's "record of a failure"[19] so Galloway pronounced the tradition of legal positivism specifically associated with Kelsen and Hart ("traditional jurisprudence") "dead", as we were urged to learn from its fatal misconceptions and errors.[20] By his own admission Galloway's account was "both polemical and perhaps exaggerated" and left open the possibility that traditional jurisprudence was not so irreversibly *in extremis* that it could not be resuscitated. Alternatively, taking it to have passed from this world to the next, Galloway saw no reason why "its soul may not transmigrate, and assume a different form".[21] This colourful rhetoric belied the serious concerns of commentators. The overriding question at the time—which may still legitimately be asked—was this. How could any strand of contemporary legal theory, if it was at all concerned to portray law as a social phenomenon, possibly have disregarded major writings, and trends, in social theory? For instance, even in contemporary analytical jurisprudence Weber's *Economy and Society*[22] can scarcely be regarded, overall, as a major source of inspiration. Were it not for Kelsen's

[18] See Donald C Galloway, "The Axiology of Analytical Jurisprudence: A Study of the Underlying Sociological Assumptions and Ideological Predilections", in Thomas W Bechtler (ed.), *Law in a Social Context: Liber Amicorum Honouring Professor Lon L. Fuller* (Kluwer, The Netherlands, 1978), 76.

[19] *CL*, 80. Hart uses "surgical" and "medical" imagery at various points in *The Concept of Law*: e.g. section 3 of ch. VI is devoted to the "pathology of a legal system". "Pathology" is also mentioned at 118, whilst at 122 Hart refers to "the pathology and embryology of legal systems".

[20] Galloway, above at n. 18, at 98.

[21] Ibid.

[22] Max Weber, *Economy and Society. An Outline of Interpretive Sociology* (Bedminster Press Inc., New York, 1968).

principled opposition to "syncretism" his "neglect" by one discipline of major developments in a significant related discipline might have been described, perhaps, as scientific myopia. But how sociologically "isolationist" *was* Hart's approach in *The Concept of Law*? And is it fair to describe Kelsen's theoretical orientation in the *Pure Theory of Law*, in particular his eschewal of disciplines such as sociology, as scientifically "myopic"? These are important, and still valid, questions bearing as they do on the work of two of the most celebrated twentieth century jurists.

[handwritten margin note: From: 1. Social theory 2. Sociological movement in law 3. Empirical sociology]

Issues explored in this book

It is convenient to divide the aims of this book into primary and secondary aims.

Primary Aim

The primary aim of this book is to revisit the main theme of what I have referred to as the "isolationism debate" in order to reach a view as to *some* sense—not necessarily the only sense—in which *The Concept of Law* might be regarded as "an essay in descriptive sociology" or simply an essay *in sociology*. I thus aim to examine, or to reassess, some of the ways in which Hart's theory genuinely engages with—in *some* sense—"sociology". For reasons to be clarified I intend to put forward classical *Weberian* sociology as a benchmark of what I mean by "sociology" for purposes of the discussion to follow. In pursuing the question of how *The Concept of Law* might be regarded as an essay in sociology, it is not intended somehow to rewrite Hart's theory within a sociological frame of reference. The overarching rationale of this book is to develop the *rudiments* of a sociological perspective on state law and legal theory. It draws upon the reservoir of insight afforded by Weber's sociological and juristic writings as a context in which to explore themes arising or selectively developed from a critical reassessment of key aspects of *The Concept of Law*. Limitations of space preclude any detailed examination of Kelsen's *Pure Theory of Law* although I will make reference to Kelsen's theory at points where it assists the overall discussion.

9

Secondary Aim

A secondary aim—albeit, perhaps, the *raison d'être* of the book—
is to explore and follow through some of the consequences of the
critical reassessment of *The Concept of Law* that follows in chapter 4. The critique is structured around three problematical areas,
or "Gordian Knots" as I propose to call them. The Gordian
Knots—I will argue—are essentially deficiencies and weaknesses
in particular aspects of *The Concept of Law*: matters of misplaced
emphasis and other elements that, I will seek to show, have
obscured fundamental aspects of a perceived social reality.

Under the First Gordian Knot, for instance, I will argue that
relatively recent accusations of intellectual and political conservatism directed towards Hart have derived from a failure (by
Hart) to place beyond doubt that the theoretical perspective or
point of view which he adopted in *The Concept of Law* was, consciously or otherwise, that of an institutional insider. As Alan
Hunt has commented, "internal" legal theory is "internal" in a
number of different but related senses. At a general level it sees
law through the eyes of judges and lawyers so the questions
which it addresses are those that concern lawyers. Thus, "the
preoccupation with how judges either do or should carry out
their judicial function narrows or restricts the scope of "legal
theory" to little more than the theory of the judicial decision".[23]
Crucially, this approach "goes hand in hand with the adoption
of the *standpoint or perspective of judges or lawyers as defining the
field of inquiry for legal theory*. Nothing that passes as legal theory has ever, to the best of my knowledge, adopted a victim or
defendant perspective".[24] Every scientific endeavour adheres to
conventions, or explicitly or tacitly adopts presuppositions,
about what it is that is the object of its investigations. This serves
to delimit one scientific realm from another. A general theory of
law attempts to formulate a position on what constitutes the dis-

[23] See Alan Hunt, "The Critique of Law: What is 'Critical' about Critical
Legal Theory?", in Peter Fitzpatrick and Alan Hunt (eds), *Critical Legal Studies*
(Basil Blackwell Ltd., Oxford, 1987), 10.

[24] Ibid., (emphasis added). But see, generally, David Dyzenhaus, *Judging the
Judges, Judging Ourselves: Truth, Reconciliation and the Apartheid Legal Order*
(Hart Publishing, Oxford, 1998).

tinctive world of the legal—of institutional structures, courts, prisons, police, coercive mechanisms of the state, legislators, legal norms and legal concepts. It is especially important for a critical theory of law to develop such a position in order to say of the legal world as so constituted: it is repressive or iniquitous, protective or corrupting, just or unjust, conducive to dissidence or to peace and stability, and so on. This—and indeed the perspectival traps, or errors of viewpoint, that I will argue have tarnished *The Concept of Law*—suggest the need for an appropriate and defensible point of view. I propose to argue that authoritative ascriptions of institutional meaning—the "legal meaning" of human actions and legally significant events ascribed on the basis of conclusive findings of fact and authoritative interpretation of law—may be figuratively conceived as emanating from a hierarchically ultimate judge of an imaginary legal system sitting in the final court of appeal: the court beyond which no further appeals can be made. For purposes of the discussion I will refer to this "ideal" supreme court judge—based around Weber's notion of the ideal type—as *Iudex*.[25] In principle, it is intended to present the realm of the legal as relatively autonomous and *analytically separable*, though not *empirically severable*, from the realm of the non-legal through the use of the theoretical construct *Iudex*. The viewpoint of *Iudex* is "institutional" in a special sense to be considered in chapter 6. But the *Iudexian* viewpoint is merely an explicit rendition of an institutional viewpoint: an "internal" viewpoint, to use Alan Hunt's expression. There is nothing to prevent such a viewpoint from existing alongside other points of view, such as that of a persecuted minority group, or of the child, or of a political dissident.

Under the Second Gordian Knot I will seek to show that it is a significant weakness of the conception of law advanced by Hart that the legal system is portrayed "as" legal rules. This approach is exemplified in formulaic aphorisms such as Hart's: "[I]n the combination of these two types of rule there lies what Austin wrongly claimed to have found in the notion of coercive

---

[25] Celtic legal history tells of a legal official, the *judex*, who acted in a quasi-judicial role. See David M Walker, *A Legal History of Scotland* (W. Green & Son Ltd., Edinburgh, 1988), Vol. I, 224.

orders, namely, 'the key to the science of jurisprudence'".[26] A standpoint such as this tends to obscure a common sense—possibly even a student textbook—account of "legal system" as a system of courts tribunals, and other organised structures engaged, among other things, in the activities of *administering and applying* a system of legal rules. In fixing upon a notion of legal system "as" a framework of legal rules there are few concessions to the possibility of a dualism of, on one hand, the ideative component of law—conceptual artefacts such as legal rules—and, on the other hand, the interactional component of law, constituted by distinct forms of human behaviour—legal institutional structures such as courts, police and prisons. The activities, behaviours and motivations of human beings working within the legal process—other than, perhaps, abstract legal reasoning processes associated with the adjudicatory function—do not feature as a major object of enquiry in *The Concept of Law*. Still less is there sustained consideration of the activities, behaviours and motivations of those "private individuals" to whom laws apply.

A further enquiry to be pursued is that of the sense and extent to which legal rules feature as a component of "social systems", using a Weber-inspired idea of "social system" derived from the writings of the sociologist Talcott Parsons. I intend to explore the role that legal rules play in structuring processes of social action or interaction. In chapter 6 I will consider a range of issues bearing on, or giving context to, that question, including the nature and structure of Weber's concept of social action and related concepts of social interaction (Talcott Parsons) and social relationship. I will examine the role of rules or norms as part of the meaningful content of social action, social interaction and the social relationship drawing, at appropriate points, on Hart's concept of "social rule"; and I will explore linkages between structural features of Weber's concept of social action and structural features of the social norm.

The Third Gordian Knot is related to the Second in that the notion of a legal system "as" rules has obscured the possibility

[26] *CL,* 81.

of viewing key aspects of law as *activities*: specific institutional activities which, merely to an extent, are rule-governed. More importantly, though, it has obscured the *relational* dimension of human behaviour and in so doing has de-emphasised one of its most fundamental dynamics: social power. Law is a significant repository of social power claiming, in most cases, a virtual monopoly on the use of force within a political community. The social power dimension of relationality in the legal context is not seriously explored in *The Concept of Law*, despite Hart's apparent commitment to "sociological" enquiry. The *ideative* processes of social power—not factual coercion, although that too is important—are a key component of the practical efficacy of a legal system. Everyone in the first instance is potentially an enforcer of legal rights against every potential duty-bearer, irrespective of the existence of coercive apparatuses which are designed to secure compliance with legal norms.[27] In the course of the discussion I will suggest that the legal relationship—not the legal rule—may properly be regarded as a primary unit of *social* thinking or sociological theorising about law. By focusing on legal relationships rather than legal rules it is possible to attain an insight into the essentially social nature of legal phenomena. Legal relationships, as the American jurist W N Hohfeld recognised, in their most abstract and irreducible form are structured as correlatives: of right↔duty and power↔liability.[28] Relationality in both the non-legal and legal contexts is part of meaningful social behaviour. Human beings ascribe meaning (*Sinn*, as Weber terms it) to their behaviour and to the behaviour of others: e.g., good, bad, moral, immoral, worthy, unworthy, and so on. They conceive of their position *vis-à-vis* others in

[27] Weber remarks that it is possible to conceive of the whole system of modern private law as the decentralisation of "domination"—in the sense of a relational power to issue "commands"—in the hands of those to whom legal rights are accorded. See Weber, *ES*, 942; Max Weber, *Max Weber on Law in Economy and Society* (Harvard University Press, Cambridge, Mass., 1954) (*LES*), 323–4.

[28] See, generally, Wesley Newcomb Hohfeld, *Fundamental Legal Conceptions as Applied in Judicial Reasoning* (Yale University Press, 4th Printing, 1966). The use of a two-way arrow here and elsewhere in this book is intended to accentuate the correlativity of "Hohfeldian" legal relationships in terms of which one legal concept (e.g. right) implies the other (duty), and *vice versa*.

relational terms: as "relationships". In the legal context individuals similarly ascribe meaning by reference to legal norms and, again, in relational terms. But sociologically significant ascriptions of meaning—that is, ascriptions of meaning which may be a particular focus of interest for sociological jurisprudence—are also made by courts of law. For example, the existence of a contractual relationship or a finding of innocence or guilt in the criminal law context are ascriptions of meaning—authoritative findings of the court—on which the mobilisation of coercive organs of the state is predicated. The conceptual structuring or reconstituting of legally relevant facts and behaviour in relational terms—for example, the ascription of rights and duties to legal persons—is treated in the discussion to follow as a function of the judicial role. But at the same time it is recognised that ascriptions of meaning by individuals other than those (such as judges) occupying official roles within institutional structures are not irrelevant to sociological enquiry or necessarily lacking in theoretical interest or significance.

A point of departure

An enquiry into the relationship between "sociology" and *The Concept of Law* (looked upon as an essay "in sociology") necessitates a standpoint on what is to count as "sociology". So far as Hart is concerned it has been recognised that his adoption of a variant of the idea that it is possible to understand social actions as they are meaningful to the actors, appears to have been "filtered wholly or in part through his reading of Winch": i.e., Peter Winch, *The Idea of a Social Science*.[29] In his book Winch gives some prominence to Weber as the focus of his critical discussion of the philosophy of the social sciences. Although some doubt has been expressed as to whether Hart actually *read* Weber,[30] the fact that Hart's writing—particularly *The Concept*

[29] See MacCormick, above at n. 6, at 166, n. 34. MacCormick's reference is to Peter Winch, *The Idea of a Social Science and its Relation to Philosophy* (Routledge & Kegan Paul Ltd., London, 1958), 57–65.

[30] See Wayne Morrison, *Jurisprudence: From the Greeks to Post-modernism* (Cavendish Publishing, London, 1997), at 371.

of Law—is highly Weberian in significant respects to be commented upon later in this book lends some credence to the approach adopted in the enquiry to follow.

But there is a possibly more compelling reason for examining linkages between Weberian sociology and Hartian legal theory. Weber's position as an acknowledged "founding father" of the discipline of sociology might have been regarded as reason enough for treating part of his work as a benchmark of what is to count as "sociology" for purposes of our enquiry. But Weber's wide-ranging interests in his *Sociology of Law* demonstrate that he was immersed in the legal literature of his time. It seems unusual nowadays for anyone to profess anything other than "expertise" in one chosen discipline, such is the departmentalisation of the modern approach to science and learning. Weber's outlook, however, was polymathic and interdisciplinary and this has important implications for the present discussion. Weber's sociological approach was applied to *law* as a social phenomenon. Significantly, Weber adopts a "sociological point of view" in the *Sociology of Law*.[31] (That viewpoint is examined in some detail in chapter 5.) As a jurist in his own right Weber's jurisprudential orientation informed his sociology of law. Weber was neither merely a sociologist writing about law nor a jurist writing about social phenomena. He occupied and combined both roles and had a unique insight into the demands of both disciplines in relation to—using Kelsen's expression—the object of cognition: law. If the very possibility of a sociological approach to law is realised in Weber, arguably there can scarcely be a better reason—in the context of an enquiry as to whether that possibility might *also* have been realised in Hart—for turning to Weber as a point of departure.

---

[31] Weber, *LES*, above at n. 27, at 11.

2

Max Weber's Science of Social Action

"Sociology . . . is a science which attempts the interpretive understanding of social action in order thereby to arrive at a causal explanation of its course and effects. In 'action' is included all human
behaviour when and in so far as the acting individual attaches a subjective meaning to it." *Max Weber*[1]

Max Weber as social and legal theorist

During the course of the twentieth century Max Weber
(1864–1920) came to be regarded as unquestionably the greatest
social theorist of the modern age. He arguably remains unrivalled
as a theoretician in the epistemology and methodology of the social
sciences. Although Weber died around eighty years ago the perva-
siveness of his writings is scarcely diminished in the many fields to
which he directed his attention: social and political theory, history,
comparative religion, economics, art, literature, the philosophy and
methodology of the social sciences, and the sociology of law.

[1] Max Weber, *The Theory of Social and Economic Organization* (The Free
Press, New York, 1947) (*TSEO*), 88. See also Max Weber, *Economy and Society.
An Outline of Interpretive Sociology* (Bedminster Press Inc., New York, 1968)
(*ES*), 4. For Weber, the acting *individual* is the "basic unit" of (social) scientific
research. As Weber says, in *TSEO*, 101: "Action in the sense of subjectively
understandable orientation of behaviour exists only as the behaviour of one or
more *individual* human beings". The social universe, therefore, is to be conceived as the sum total of component individuals. Collectivities such as the state
or the corporation are thus treated as the resultants and modes of organisation
of the particular acts of individual persons. For a discussion of the postulate of
methodological individualism (as it has come to be known), see further Steven
Lukes, "Methodological Individualism Reconsidered" (1968) 19 *British Journal
of Sociology* 119.

According to Alan Hunt, "Weber's presence insinuates itself into nearly every important debate and controversy within sociology".[2] In the first part of his monumental work, *Wirtschaft und Gesellschaft* (*Economy and Society*),[3] which was published posthumously, Weber attempted, among other things, to develop a systematic exposition of sociological concepts and methodological principles. It is towards this part of his work in particular that significant scholarly attention is directed in contemporary social theory. Weber's position as a jurist, and in particular as a sociologist of law, is also worth acknowledging in the present context.

The Sociology of Law

Weber was trained as a lawyer and studied law at the University of Heidelberg, later establishing himself in Berlin as a jurist in 1891 following the publication of a paper on Roman agrarian history. The part of *Economy and Society* which constitutes his *Sociology of Law* (*Rechtssoziologie*)[4] is a testament to his extensive historical and comparative legal learning. It is instructive to note the breadth of Weber's interests in his *Sociology of Law*. Weber constructs an ideal typology of legal systems which is based on a classification of types of legal thought: formal rationality, formal irrationality, substantive rationality and substantive irrationality. He focuses particularly upon the concept of rationality in legal thinking and devotes attention to the unique type of legal rationality that has evolved in western culture. He classifies fields of substantive law according to conventionally held distinctions: for example, public law and private law, "government" and "administration", criminal law and private law, and tort and crime. He devotes a substantial chapter to the various social and economic conditions which lead to the creation of legal rights. He undertakes a comparative study of legal professionals ("legal *honoratiores*") and attempts to establish linkages between professional legal training and the emergence of types of legal thought. Finally (according only to *this* overview), Weber considers

---

[2] Alan Hunt, *The Sociological Movement in Law* (MacMillan Press, 1978), 93.

[3] Weber, *ES*, above at n. 1.

[4] The *Rechtssoziologie* has been published separately as *Max Weber on Law in Economy and Society* (Harvard University Press, Cambridge, Mass., 1954) (*LES*).

the embeddedness in legal processes of "superiority" or "legitimate authority" (which Weber's translators have termed "domination", being a translation from the German "*Herrschaft*"), and he discusses the manifestations of such power in ordinary legal relationships.

It would be of no practical utility to attempt to summarise here Weber's *Sociology of Law* because the complexity of treatment of the subject matter and density of Weber's writing defies ready simplification. Our primary interest in any event is not in Weber's *Sociology of Law*, as such, but in his general sociology. Yet although it is beyond the scope of this book to focus in depth on Weber's *Sociology of Law* the sociology is a valuable reference source in applying, and formulating a technique for applying, Weber's general sociology to law. The *sociological point of view* which Weber outlines—and which is discussed in chapter 5—is an especially useful analytical tool.

As a preliminary exercise, then, it is instructive to examine the philosophical context in which Weber's approach to sociology and the sociology of law was located.

Philosophical influences in Weber

In *The Critique of Pure Reason*[5] Kant famously distinguished between the *phenomenal* world and the *noumenal* world. The phenomenal world was the world of external objects or events which we know by sensory perception, and the noumenal world was the intelligible world of objects of experience not given by the senses but conceived in the mind. This distinction formed the philosophical basis of two strands of late nineteenth century German philosophy, exponents of which—all contemporaries of Weber—influenced Weber in the formulation of his science of social action. Weber's writings on the epistemology and methodology of social science owes much to the work of Wilhelm Dilthey, a philosopher and historian in the German Idealist tradition, and philosophers Heinrich Rickert and Wilhelm Windelband, both representatives of the Southwest German school of Neo-Kantianism. Yet, characteristically, Weber adopted positions which at points were completely at variance with their teachings.

[5] Immanuel Kant, *The Critique of Pure Reason* (Chicago: Encyclopaedia Brittanica, 1952, translated by J M D Meiklejohn).

Origin of the Approach to Interpretive Understanding

Dilthey based his approach on the recognition that the subject matter of the mental sciences (*Geisteswissenschaften*) as he called them, differs from the subject matter of the natural sciences (*Naturwissenschaften*). According to this view the natural sciences were basically concerned with such matters as the investigation of the properties and structure of matter (including living matter in the biological sense) and energy, and with changes which those phenomena undergo, in accordance with scientific "laws" defining these properties derived from such investigation. Mental sciences, on the other hand, dealt with the study of "mankind". Human beings act "meaningfully". They ascribe meaning to their actions in pursuing goals, interpreting the behaviour of others as a basis for their own action, evaluating their actions and following rules. Knowledge of that, Dilthey maintained, was possible only through experience (*Erleben*) and understanding (*Verstehen*), achieved through a process of re-experiencing or re-living (*Nacherleben*) the meanings intended by historical actors. Thus, experience was to be understood from within, while the world of physical matter was conceived from without. The study of human behaviour had to recognise the sense in which the inner nature of the individual, the world of the mind, affects that behaviour: "Only in the world of the mind which creatively, responsibly and autonomously, stirs within us, has life its value, its goal and its meaning".[6]

The critical element of Dilthey's distinction between natural sciences and mental sciences lay in the proposition that the methods of the natural sciences were neither adequate nor appropriate to the task of acquiring knowledge of human beings and their behaviour. For, in the natural sciences—so the argument went—knowledge is based on the observation, categorisation and quantification of externally observable phenomena. By contrast, the knowledge or understanding of human beings and their behaviour had to proceed from an intuitive grasp of internal phenomena, represented as inner experience. For Dilthey it was legitimate for science to consider the world of the mind in order to reach an understanding of

[6] From H P Rickman (ed. and trans.), *W. Dilthey Selected Writings* (Cambridge University Press, 1976) 172.

humankind. The world of the mind is first of all determined by the world of experience, and it becomes legitimate to make "objects" of the mind the subject of judgments and theoretical discussion, since these are all part of the reality of human experience. Thus Dilthey considered that the "acquired structure of mental life" which includes valuations and purposes affecting a person's behaviour, colouring ideas and states, organising impressions and regulating emotions, should be abstracted from the pattern of life. It should be called "the mental" and made the subject of judgments and theoretical discussion.[7] The investigator wishing to understand the meanings intended by an actor could approach the problem of bridging the gap between his or her own intuitive experience and that of the actor under investigation by entering into a type of empathic liaison with the actor, through careful introspection and a "projection" into the actor's "expressions".

In Dilthey's sense, "expressions" referred to any manifestation of mental content. These could include actions of any type, facial expressions, gestures, movements and exclamations, or words and sentences.[8] The process of empathising, re-living or re-experiencing which led to "higher understanding" of a given actor as a methodological approach was thought to depend to a large extent on the experiences which the *investigator* had undergone. The more those experiences corresponded, even if only approximately, with those of the subject of the investigation, the more enlightened would be the investigator's understanding.

Origin of the Approach to Causal Explanation

While Weber accepted much of Dilthey's teaching, particularly his espousal of the method of *Verstehen* or interpretive understanding and its processes of empathising and re-living, in his own approach he adopted a position which opposed Dilthey's rejection of the possibility of positivistic methods (i.e., those appropriate to the natural sciences) being applied in the study of human behaviour. The observation of regular relations between external events and uniformities and the drawing of appropriate inferences from these, in Weber's view, had to be taken hand in hand with the attribution to

[7] Ibid., 170–1.
[8] Ibid., 218, 221–2.

actors of subjective meanings and the interpretive understanding of action which emerged from that process. Commentators have noted that for Weber, interpretive explanations had to become causal explanations in order to reach the "dignity" of a scientific proposition. Empathy (*Einfuehlung*) and reliving were only facilitating processes. *Verstehen* and causal explanation had to be regarded as "correlative" rather than opposed principles of method in the social sciences: "Immediate intuitions of meaning can be transformed into valid knowledge only if they can be incorporated into theoretical structures that aim at causal explanation".[9]

Although Weber stressed the interdependence of the processes of interpretive understanding and causal explanation, he failed to elaborate the notion of causal explanation in detail. This has made it difficult to imagine how it could be applied as a practical technique. What is certain, though, is that Weber's notion of causality is cast in terms of *probability*. Definitions and formulae expressed in probabilistic terms occur frequently in Weber's work. Thus for Weber, "causal explanation depends on being able to determine that there is a probability . . . that a given observable event (overt or subjective) will be followed or accompanied by another event".[10]

The Neo-Kantian philosophers Heinrich Rickert and Wilhelm Windelband also exerted a powerful influence on Weber. They differed from Dilthey in locating the distinction between methods appropriate respectively to the study of human behaviour and natural phenomena, not in necessities arising from differences of subject matter but in terms of method or approach to that subject matter. They held, as Weber did, that human behaviour *could* in appropriate cases be studied by the methods of natural science just as, in other cases, the so-called cultural sciences or *Kulturwissenschaften* approach was more appropriate. Weber's radical approach demanded, in a sense, a combining of both approaches. The distinction to be drawn between *Kulturwissenschaften* and *Naturwissenschaften* lay in the fact that in the former—for example, history, jurisprudence, sociology—so-called *idiographic* sciences, the approach was to particularise the subject matter. This method con-

[9] Lewis A Coser, *Masters of Sociological Thought: Ideas in Historical and Social Context* (Harcourt Brace Jovanovich Inc., 2nd ed. 1977), 220–1.
[10] *TSEO*, 99.

centrated on the uniqueness of historical actors or events. In the latter—for example, chemistry, biology, physics—so-called *nomothetic* sciences, the approach was to abstract and generalise. The objective was to formulate universal "laws" capable of subsuming all specific manifestations of phenomena within their scope.

The Doctrines of Value-Relevance and Value-Freedom

In *opposition* to the Neo-Kantians, however, Weber argued that scientific methodology, proceeding by way of generalisation and abstraction, was equally valid for cultural sciences as for the natural sciences. The formulation of sociological *concepts*, such as the ideal type, proceeded from an observation of the concrete action of particular actors. It then sought to generalise and establish relationships transcending the particularity of subjective meaning and individual action present in observed instances. Secondary literature on Weber emphasises the role of the social scientist to generalise from random and unique aspects of the reality under consideration. Concrete individual actions are conceived as "cases" or "instances" to be subsumed under theoretical generalisations. The individualising approach *neglects* generic elements and concentrates attention on particular features of phenomena or concrete historical actors.[11] What this requires is a method which allows a selection to be made from the infinite variety of empirical reality. This is where Rickert's influence on Weber was most marked. In his doctrine of *value-relevance (Wertbeziehung)*, Rickert asserted that empirical reality as presented to the senses is both infinite and inexhaustible in space and in time. As secondary literature emphasises, the number of possible objects of perception is infinitely great, and any such object may be subdivided into an infinite number of lesser objects. Each of these differs from the others at least by its place in space and time.[12]

It was necessary, according to Rickert, for the historian to make a choice or selection from the boundlessness of reality in terms of *values* which guided that selection, according to a criterion of *significance*. What made a particular object of cognition significant

[11] See, generally, Coser, above at n. 9, at 219–20.

[12] See H H Bruun, *Science, Values and Politics in Max Weber's Methodology* (Munksgaard, Copenhagen, 1972), 85.

23

was the relationship in which it stood to objective or universally acknowledged cultural values. This value relation—as historians of sociology have noted—would permit a selection from the infinite multiplicity of reality only if the values entering into the value relation were universally acknowledged cultural values. *Against* Rickert, Weber took the view that the values which governed the selection of phenomena and their abstraction from infinite reality were not universally acknowledged cultural values, but those of the investigator, influenced by the type of problems under investigation, the particular nature of the subject matter, and the questions which required to be answered. Those matters could never readily be contained within objective cultural values, and depended very much on the investigator's own calculations of significance. Weber's commentators have noted that there were no intrinsically scientific criteria of selection. Every investigator must pursue his or her own moral stance, but that need not detract from social scientific objectivity. Talcott Parsons argues that guidance is given through the explicit or implicit application of a "formal schema of proof" which is independent of any value system "except the value of scientific proof". This makes possible the establishment of causal relations between a descriptively given phenomenon and either its antecedents or its consequences.[13]

The notion of value-relevance is distinguishable from Weber's postulate of *value-freedom*. What Weber meant by this was that the social scientist, having selected an object of enquiry, could not allow personal preferences or prejudices, or political or religious beliefs, to colour his or her judgment or contaminate any of the conclusions reached with respect to that object. For Weber, the more a social scientist approximated to a position of value-neutrality or value-freedom, the more scientifically "true" or objective were the results of the investigation. Scientific objectivity demanded that the investigator should reach out beyond personal values and present a view that is neutral in relation to those values.[14]

---

[13] Coser, above at n. 9, at 221 (quoting Talcott Parsons, *The Structure of Social Action* (The Free Press, New York, 1958), 594).

[14] See Talcott Parsons, "Value-Freedom and Objectivity", in Otto Stammer (ed.), *Max Weber and Sociology Today* (Basil Blackwell, Oxford, 1971), 33.

While accepting Rickert's view of the boundlessness of reality and the need for selection and choice in scientific investigation, Weber opposed Rickert's insistence on the particularising approach of *Kulturwissenschaften* by adopting a position in which a *generalising* approach could be combined with the processes of selection and abstraction contained within the notion of value-relevance. For Weber, this justified the social scientist's formulating and using sociological concepts. Starting from the idea of a boundless reality it followed that a scientific reproduction of the whole of reality was practically and logically impossible. All scientific disciplines therefore, consciously or unconsciously, had to make use of concepts that could only embrace *parts* of reality. This is the point at which Weber's concept of the *ideal type*, considered later in this chapter, entered the picture. What may be noted for the moment is that the content of the ideal type depended on the investigator's judgments of significance and on the problems, questions and specialities necessitated, on the one hand, by the subject matter, and on the other hand, by the investigator's particular objectives.

Max Weber's science of social action

Many of the philosophical undercurrents which I have touched upon find more detailed expression in Weber's science of social action. Weber's definition of "sociology" makes its appearance at an early stage in Part I of *Economy and Society* and is followed by a lengthy elaboration in numbered observations. The definition shows how the constituent parts of Weber's sociology dovetail with one another:[15]

> "Sociology (in the sense in which this highly ambiguous word is used here) is a science which attempts the interpretive understanding of social action in order thereby to arrive at a causal explanation of its course and effects. In 'action' is included all human behaviour when and in so far as the acting individual attaches a subjective meaning to it. . . . Action is social in so far as, by virtue of the subjective meaning attached to it by the acting individual (or individuals), it takes account of the behaviour of others and is thereby oriented in its course".

[15] *TSEO*, 88.

Subjective Meaning

The subjective meaning of social action stands in a relationship to the complex of motivating ideas which impel that action. Dilthey observes that there is a regular relation between an action and some mental content which allows probable inferences to be drawn. In a general sense, an actor might be said to orient his or her action consciously or purposively towards the attainment of a certain end subjectively represented in advance of its attainment by an idea in the actor's mind. That is perhaps most clearly manifested in goal-oriented or purposive action. Action may be only partially explicable by reference to a subjective meaning-content identified as a motive for action. For instance action that is oriented by reference to a norm or "ought" proposition can seldom be accounted meaningful *exhaustively* by reference to that norm.

Weber distinguishes two kinds of subjective meaning: (i) the actual existing meaning in the given concrete case of a particular actor, or the average or approximate meaning attributable to a plurality of actors, and (ii) the theoretically conceived pure type of subjective meaning attributed to a hypothetical actor in a given type of action.[16] The latter category of meaning—a pure or idealised attribution of meaning—is a theoretical abstraction. Since it is "ideal" it need not correspond to the subjective meaning present in a concrete instance. Being theoretical, it may involve generality and attribution of meanings of the first category: a "synthesis" of concrete individual phenomena, giving an account of common features present across a generality of similar though individual cases. Weber emphasises that "meaning" does not refer to an objectively "correct" meaning or one which is "true" in some metaphysical sense. There is no true or valid meaning, but only one which seems appropriate in the light of the data with which the investigator is working. On the other hand scientific objectivity demands that the meaning ascribed by the investigator should be at least consistent with all the evidence presented and from which any necessary inferences may be drawn. As Weber insists: "All interpretation of meaning, like all scientific observation, strives for clarity and verifiable accuracy of insight and comprehension".[17]

[16] *TSEO*, 89.
[17] Ibid., 90.

Weber argues that subjective meaning is most clearly grasped when action is *zweckrational* or purpose-rational: purposively oriented to a certain end. Because it involves consciously weighing up means and ends this type of action possesses for the investigator the highest degree of verifiable certainty. The investigator places meaning in an inclusive context (*Sinnzusammenhang*). Weber imagines the example of a person writing down the proposition twice two equals four: "Understanding in this sense is attained if we know that he is engaged in balancing a ledger or in making a scientific demonstration, or is engaged in some other task of which this particular act would be an appropriate part".[18] The adequacy of interpretation of a complex of subjective meaning relative to a course of conduct is assessed according to the "habitual modes of thought and feeling" of the investigator. Meaning is "adequate" when it is judged to be "typical" or "correct". Weber links the requirement of meaning adequacy to a requirement of causal adequacy, which is the requirement that, according to established generalisations from experience, there should be a probability that a sequence of events will always actually occur in the same way. For Weber meaning adequacy and causal adequacy are *both* necessary for a correct causal interpretation of a concrete and a typical course of action.

Weber gives an example of action that may be accounted meaningful in terms of the relation which it bears to *norms* functioning as a motivating influence. He calls this type of social action *Gesellschaftshandeln* (rationally regulated or associative action).[19] A major component is meaningful orientation towards rules. Elsewhere Weber refers more explicitly to the normative component of subjective meaning, identifying two senses in which a rule of purposive action would have a bearing on empirical knowledge of an actor's behaviour.[20] First, it may require to be considered as a real determinant of empirical action. Secondly, it would be taken into account as an element in the stock of knowledge and concepts with which the investigator approaches the enquiry. The investigator's

[18] Ibid., 95.

[19] *ES*, 1376.

[20] Max Weber, "The Concept of 'Following a Rule'", in W G Runciman (ed.), *Max Weber, Selections in Translation* (Cambridge University Press, 1978), ch. 5. See esp. 105.

knowledge of the ideally possible "meaning" of the action makes it possible to have empirical knowledge of the action. Weber notes that in the empirical sphere the norm is undoubtedly one determinant of the course of events, but from the logical point of view it is *only* one. According to Weber there can be a whole range of degrees of consciousness of the influence exerted on action by determinants such as these.

Social Action

The frame of reference within which Weber theorises about human social behaviour is that of *social action*. It has two aspects. First, as we have seen, action includes all human behaviour when and in so far as the acting individual attaches a subjective meaning to it. Secondly, action is social in so far as, by virtue of the subjective meaning attached to it, it takes account of the behaviour of others and is thereby oriented in its course. Action is either overt or purely inward or subjective. Purely subjective action in this sense is inaccessible to sociological enquiry unless in some sense objectified by an externally perceptible "expression", to use Dilthey's term. Language, of course, is the most obvious and powerful form of "expression", enabling communication—the intersubjective exchange of ideas—between or among human beings.

The external and internal facets of human action are accessible to sociological enquiry, as Weber recognises, because on one hand action is always "external". In this sense one might say that it had brought about a change in the "real world". Action is thus seen to interfere with the course of nature. But on the other hand action arises from within in the sense that ideas motivate action. If therefore it is possible to link the observation of some manifested mental content (e.g., an action such as a verbal utterance which reveals an intention to act in a particular way) with a subsequent action which is apparently the carrying into effect of the intention so expressed, we might perceive in this a causal relationship which links the manifested mental content (an "event" in Weber's terms) with the resultant action (another "event").

For Weber, action is rationally oriented to a system of discrete individual ends when the end, the means and the secondary results are all rationally taken into account and weighed. A type of rationally oriented action with a significant normative component has already been briefly mentioned: rationally regulated or associative action (*Gesellschaftshandeln*). This type of action is dependent upon rules as a reference point for orientation of the action. Weber outlines its principal features as follows:[21]

> "Social action is Gesellschaftshandeln (rationally regulated action) insofar as it is (1) meaningfully oriented toward rules which have been (2) established rationally with a view toward the expected behavior of the 'associates' (Vergesellschaftete), and insofar as (3) the meaningful orientation is indeed instrumentally rational on the part of the actor."

Gesellschafts-handeln [handwritten marginal note]

The rationale underlying the legislative task—in other words, the role of the legislator in the law-creation process—can be said to take as its point of departure the assumption that those to whom the enacted laws apply will in fact largely orient their action by reference to those laws, e.g., "obey" the laws. It is assumed that they will act instrumentally rationally in avoiding punishment or whatever other disadvantage may flow from non-compliance.

Interpretive Understanding

Attaining an interpretive understanding (*Verstehen*) of the subjective meaning of a course of action can involve, as practical methods, empathising with the actor under investigation or imaginatively reliving concrete experiences. As Dilthey observed, the investigator may "project" into the outward expressions of the actor which manifest some metal content: acts, thoughts, gestures, and so on. For Weber, empathy plays only a facilitating role in this process. It is not an essential condition of meaningful interpretation. The emotional context in which the action took place is also important. Emotional reactions such as anxiety, anger, ambition, envy, jealousy, love, enthusiasm, pride, and so on may be the outward expression of certain underlying value orientations.

Weber postulates two kinds of interpretive understanding: direct observational understanding (*aktuelles Verstehen*) and explanatory understanding (*erklärendes Verstehen*). Explanatory understanding approaches "true" understanding in the Weberian sense, involving,

[21] *ES*, 1376.

as it does, the attainment of a grasp of motives for acting. Explanatory understanding seeks to find *reasons*. The requirement to place an act in an intelligible and more inclusive context of meaning refers to a plurality of elements which form a coherent whole on the level of meaning. As Parsons puts it, "There are several possible modes of meaningful relation between such elements, such as logical consistency, the aesthetic harmony of a style, or the appropriateness of means to an end".[22] According to Weber, the act must be placed in an understandable sequence of motivation, the understanding of which can be treated as an explanation of the actual course of behaviour. As we have seen, explanatory understanding must also be scientifically validated by explanation in terms of *causal* factors. Unless this is done the method of *Verstehen* is only a source of hypotheses about human action. As Weber says:[23]

> "Every interpretation attempts to attain clarity and certainty, but no matter how clear an interpretation as such appears to be from the point of view of meaning, it cannot on this account alone claim to be the causally valid interpretation. On this level it must remain only a peculiarly plausible hypothesis."

Verification of subjective interpretation by comparison with the concrete course of events is, in Weber's view, indispensable.

Causal Explanation

According to Kurt Wolff, what is significant about Weber's notion of sociology is that:[24]

> ". . . for Max Weber sociology is an enterprise which both interprets or understands (namely, meanings) and (causally) explains (namely, events in time); moreover, which interprets in order to be able to explain; which, as it were, prepares by interpretation its candidates for causal explanation. That is to say, Max Weber thought that before we can ask causal questions calling for explanation, we must understand what we want to ask causal questions about; we must be

[22] *TSEO*, 95, n. 13.

[23] See ibid., 96–7.

[24] Kurt H Wolff, "Phenomenology and Sociology", in Tom Bottomore and Robert Nisbet (eds.), *A History of Sociological Analysis* (Heinemann Educational Books Ltd., London, 1978), 501.

able to interpret it. Thus, logically, understanding precedes explaining".

The object of the sociological investigation is the correct causal interpretation of a concrete, or typical, course of action. The end result of Weberian sociological enquiry is explanation of a certain kind: explanation in terms of the theoretical imputation of causal relationships and also explanation in terms of subjective meanings or motives. This latter type of explanation is not denoted by Weber's term "causal explanation". Yet if sociology is a science which attempts the interpretive understanding of social action *in order* to arrive at a causal explanation of its course and effects, the suggestion is that Weberian sociological explanation is, ultimately, *causal* explanation. It is tempting to infer that "causal explanation" subsumes explanation in terms of subjective meaning. That is to an extent borne out by Weber's insistence that the twin requirements of adequacy on the level of meaning and causal adequacy must be present simultaneously for a correct *causal* interpretation.[25] But, as Weber insists, even if "perfect" adequacy on the level of meaning is attained in the course of an investigation this can never compensate for a lack of adequacy on the level of causality, and *vice versa*.

As we have seen, interpretive understanding is a technique applied to internal meaningful processes: that is, purely mental complexes of meaning. There can never be perfect knowledge of the mind of another. The investigator must rely on introspection—examination of his or her own experience of what human experience in some particular context amounts to—and extrapolate from that to the experience of others in specific situations. In this way, internal meaningful processes of those others may become meaningful to the investigator. There will always be a "hiatus" between the investigator's ascription or assumption of meaning—which Weber calls "a peculiarly plausible hypothesis"—and the actual meaning present in the mind of the actor under investigation. This "hiatus", as Weber seems to suggest, can to an extent be bridged by applying a technique which is appropriate for apprehending empirically observable concrete phenomena, i.e., "events" in time. By this means, the validity of any ascription of subjective meaning

[25] *TSEO*, 99.

may be verified. Although a motive for acting or intention to act may be treated as a "cause" of the resulting action, the sociological technique of imputing cause, as Weber presents it, apparently focuses interest not on the motive or intention in itself as a cause of action, but on the external "event" by which motive or intention is manifested, for example a verbal utterance. It then seeks to establish a causal connection between that "event" and a later "event", for example an act that accords with the motive or intention so manifested. Nevertheless, we would apply the quite separate technique of interpretive understanding to, for example, the verbal utterance, treated for this purpose not as an "event" (although that is what it is), but as something possessing significance in a specifically ideative and human sense. Weber's reliance upon two techniques of explanation, one appropriate to *Geisteswissenschaften* and the other to *Naturwissenschaften*, does not mean that one technique *is* subsumed by another. They remain, on the contrary, separate and valid techniques in their own right, and applicable according to differing interests appropriate to each.

Nonetheless, the *outcome* of the process—of meaning ascription and causal imputation—is a "causal explanation" which takes account of the internal and introspective aspect of the process: yielding hypotheses about subjective meaning, such hypotheses then being verified by the external and empirical aspect of the process, that is, observation of concrete "events" which may include manifestations of mental content such as linguistic expressions. We might then say, to be more accurate, that the end result is explanation in terms of subjective meaning as verified or supported by the observation of events in time to which causal relationships are imputed.

The recognition of the interdependence of the processes of interpretive understanding and causal explanation does not assist us with the question of what causal explanation actually involves. Weber quite simply fails to elaborate his ideas in sufficient detail to enable causal explanation to be properly applied as a scientific technique. For Weber, "causal explanation depends on being able to determine that there is a probability, which in the rare ideal case can be numerically stated, but is always in some sense calculable, that a given observable event (overt or subjective) will be followed or accompanied by another event".[26] There are basically two aspects to this. First, the results of causal explanation are cast in terms of probability. Secondly, concrete phenomena are reduced to "observable events"—whether overt or subjective: the latter presumably including manifestations of some mental content—which stand in a causal relation to one another, and on a temporal continuum, the earlier event being adjudged a "cause" of the later event. Weber's predilection for "explanation" in terms of probability underlines his faith in the possibility that social science could approach mathematical precision that would elevate it to the status of "true" science. The possibility, in the "rare ideal case" of numerical statement, implies the use of statistical techniques of research. The fact that probability is involved should not lead us to suppose that the results of sociological investigation will yield anything as powerful as "certainty".

The Ideal Type

The analytical construct (*Gedankenbild*) or methodological device of the ideal type has been identified as the logical conclusion of a number of strands of thought underlying Weber's methodological writings.[27] The infinite plurality of concrete reality is for Weber, the starting point:[28]

> "Now, as soon as we attempt to reflect about the way in which life confronts us in immediate concrete situations, it presents an infinite multiplicity of successively and coexistently emerging and disappearing events, both 'within' and 'outside' ourselves. The absolute infinitude of this multiplicity is seen to remain undiminished even when our attention is focused on a single 'object', for instance, a concrete act of exchange, as soon as we seriously attempt an exhaustive description of *all* the individual components of this 'individual phenomena', to say nothing of explaining it causally."

[margin note: maybe relevant for concept of Einstellung]

[26] Ibid.

[27] Raymond Aron, *Main Currents in Sociological Thought* (Weidenfeld and Nicolson, London, 1967), 201.

[28] Max Weber, " 'Objectivity' in Social Science and Social Policy", in *Max Weber, The Methodology of the Social Sciences* (The Free Press, New York, 1949) (*OSS*), 72.

Order is brought to this "chaos" because only the *part* of an experience is significant that is related to the values with which the experience is approached. Those values influence the investigator in formulating criteria guiding the selection of phenomena of interest. I previously noted that scientific disciplines utilise concepts that embrace only part of the reality of significance to the investigator. The ideal type is such a concept. It articulates similarities occurring in a number of individual concrete phenomena. The phenomena are subsumed under the generalising terms of the concept. Each individual datum is seen as a case or an instance, or a contributory factor to a case or instance, of the generic type. According to Weber:[29]

> "An ideal type is formed by the one-sided *accentuation* of one or more points of view and by the synthesis of a great many diffuse, discrete, more or less present and occasionally absent *concrete individual* phenomena, which are arranged according to those one-sidedly emphasized viewpoints into a unified *analytical* construct (*Gedankenbild*). In its conceptual purity, this mental construct . . . cannot be found empirically anywhere in reality. It is a *utopia*."

The ideal type represents the logical conclusion of Weber's method of *Verstehen*. The investigator first attempts to ascribe subjective meaning: either the actual existing meaning in the concrete case of a particular actor, or the average or approximate meaning attributable to a plurality of actors. The data thus yielded enable the investigator to construct a theoretically conceived pure type of meaning attributable to hypothetical actors in a given type of action. The actors are "hypothetical" in the sense that the theoretically conceived meaning does not relate to any actor in particular, but incorporates similarities found across a range of typical cases. The meaning so conceived represents a synthesis of many concrete individual phenomena.

A similar procedure attends the treatment of ideal-typical causal explanation. Here, the concrete individual phenomena comprising data for inclusion in the ideal type are typical sequences of causally linked "events": pluralities of "events" that occur in "constant conjunction", to use Hume's expression. "Events" occurring in

[29] *Ibid.,* 90.

constant conjunction or regular sequence that meet the criterion of causal adequacy are candidates for inclusion in the ideal type. Established generalisations from experience yield a probability that the events will always actually occur in the same way. Such events must also correspond to typical subjective meanings. The requirements of causal adequacy and meaning adequacy must, in other words, co-exist in the ideal type.

Weber's preoccupation with rationality in human behaviour expresses itself in his preference for the incorporation of rational processes in ideal type constructs. Weber favours rational processes because the construction of a purely rational course of action serves the sociologist as a type which has the merit of comprehensibility and lack of ambiguity. Conceptual precision of sociological concepts can be achieved if the investigator strives for the highest possible degree of adequacy on the level of meaning.[30] In Weber's view, this aim is realised to a high degree if the concepts and generalisations of the ideal type formulate rational processes. The ideal type states what course action would take if it were strictly rational, unaffected by errors or emotional factors. J W N Watkins comments that the purpose of the ideal type is as a heuristic aid which tells nothing about the real world but which throws into relief the real world's deviations from the type. Hence, the ideal type may assist in the detection of disturbing factors, such as habit and tradition, which "deflect actual individuals from a rational course of action". Watkins likens this process to improving one's appreciation of the shape of a roughly circular object "by placing over it an accurate tracing of a circle".[31]

Once the investigator has expended effort in formulating an ideal type, it might be asked towards what practical ends the construct can be applied. Secondary literature on Weber maintains that an ideal type may serve the investigator as a measuring rod to ascertain similarities as well as deviations in concrete cases. Other applications of the ideal type include the most obvious—that it helps to bring "order" to "chaos". The construct may aid comparative study, facilitating the identification of defining characteristics or

---

[30] *TSEO*, 109–10.

[31] J W N Watkins, "Ideal Types and Historical Explanation", in Alan Ryan (ed.), *The Philosophy of Social Explanation* (Oxford University Press, 1973), 85.

outstanding features of specific types of social action. "Externally" the type may enable a particular course of action to be identified *as* a type, having tolerably well-defined boundaries. It may help us to form judgments about the relationship of one type of action to other types whose boundaries are similarly defined. Characteristics which are "internal" to the type may also be differentiated from peripheral elements. It may additionally serve as a model for identifying important "structural" features of a given course of action: for example, normative structures such as the constitution of a political or social entity.

Towards a sociological perspective on legal theory

The brief, much simplified and necessarily highly compressed account of Weber's science of social action outlined in this chapter is put forward as a basis for an exploration—at various places in the remainder of this book—of points of similarity or divergence between central features of Hart's theory of law and Weberian sociology. More importantly, however, it is intended to serve as a basis *in its own right* for developing or laying initial foundations for a sociological perspective on legal theory that draws on key insights from social and legal theory. In chapters 5, 6 and 7 in particular I will seek to show how certain constructively modified elements of (on one hand) Weberian sociology and (on the other) the Hartian and Hohfeldian variants of analytical jurisprudence may be combined in a way that better enhances the explanatory power of each of those fields of enquiry towards an improved understanding of the social phenomenon of law. The synoptic account of key aspects of Hart's expository jurisprudence, which follows in chapter 3, is an essential preliminary to this interdisciplinary undertaking.

3
Hart's Nucleic Expository Theory

"[I]n the combination of these two types of rule there lies what Austin wrongly claimed to have found in the notion of coercive orders, namely, 'the key to the science of jurisprudence'." *H L A Hart*[1]

Hart's approach to theory

What is the point, or purpose, of a theory of law? Why is it thought to be necessary, in pursuing the question "what is law?", to turn to a *theory of* law rather than (say) to a simple, accurate descriptive statement *about* law or definition of law? Hart argued that the question "what is law?" covertly invites a definition of the word "law" as a response. But a definition of "law" could not satisfy the quest for enlightenment, for in Hart's view the question of what law is unravels to *three* distinct but related issues or questions which focus attention on the nature of law as coercive orders and as an "affair of rules" and explore the relationship between law and morality. Hart's so-called recurrent questions are discussed in greater detail later in this chapter. Of Hart's three questions, no one question by itself could entirely dispose of the original question "what is law?", whilst each of the three was best tackled by theoretical or philosophical enquiry. The point is that for Hart nothing concise enough to be recognised as a definition could provide a satisfactory answer to the question "what is law?" given that the three underlying issues were too different from one another to yield a definition. Moreover, each of the issues required extended discursive treatment. There was thus no analytical panacea providing a ready solution to Hart's recurrent questions. It was Hart's explicit aim "to advance

[1] H L A Hart, *The Concept of Law* (Clarendon Press, Oxford, 2nd ed. 1994) (*CL*), 81.

legal *theory*" by providing an analysis of the structure of a municipal legal system and by differentiating law, coercion and morality as
types of social phenomena.[2] This was essentially Hart's manifesto
for a theory of law. The requirement for "theory" itself was taken
for granted and Hart did not dwell, in *The Concept of Law*,[3] on the
question of what legal theory is or, for that matter, what theory is
generally.

What, in a rudimentary sense, characterised Hart's theoretical
approach to law? Hart, rooted in the school of linguistic philosophy
pioneered by J L Austin, has been described by William Twining as
"anti-programmatic": there are only "interesting questions awaiting
resolution by the application of analytical acid".[4] According to
Twining, almost the only claim that is made is that "this tradition
of philosophising has developed a number of techniques of wide
application for dissolving puzzlements and exposing errors". By this
account we need not look to Hart "for coherent frames of reference".[5] Yet Hart subtly tended towards "grand theory" in his theory of law where, among other salient features, law is characterised
as the union of primary and secondary rules. This—not the competing "Austinian" notion of law as the commands or coercive
orders of a sovereign—was for Hart the "key to the science of
jurisprudence". That alone perhaps suggests a theoretical vision
that was "grander" than Twining conceded.

Key aspects of Hart's work can be described as coming within
the province of analytical jurisprudence, the focal concerns of which
include systematic and theoretical analysis: of legal concepts and
conceptions, of legal validity and efficacy of laws, of the structure
of laws and systems of laws, of the nature of legal reasoning and
legal interpretation, and of the application of logic in the law. An
important principle underlying these analytical concerns is the separation of law and morality, summarised in John Austin's aphorism,
"The existence of law is one thing; its merit or demerit is another".[6]

[2] Ibid., 17.

[3] Above at n. 1.

[4] William Twining, "Academic Law and Legal Philosophy: The Significance of
Herbert Hart" (1979) 95 *Law Quarterly Review* 557 at 569.

[5] Ibid.

[6] Austin continues: "Whether it be or be not is one enquiry; whether it be or be not
conformable to an assumed standard, is a different enquiry. A law, which actually

Hart usefully lists a number of propositions to which the expression positivism has been applied in Anglo-American literature. Among these are the contentions: that laws are commands of human beings; that there is no necessary connection between law and morals, or law "as it is" and law "as it ought to be"; that the analysis of meanings of legal concepts is to be distinguished from (but is "in no way hostile to") historical inquiries, sociological inquiries and the critical appraisal of law in terms of morals, social aims and functions; that a legal system is a "closed logical system" in which correct decisions can be deduced from predetermined legal rules by logical means alone.[7] Bentham, Austin and Kelsen were united in holding to the postulate of the separability of law "as it is" from law "as it ought to be" (the so-called "separability thesis").[8]

In the remainder of this chapter I propose to focus attention only upon what I might perhaps describe as Hart's "nucleic expository theory"—the nucleus of *The Concept of Law* which concentrates on analytical issues which include: the notion of law as a system of rules (as opposed to commands or coercive orders of a sovereign); the distinction between primary and secondary rules and the related notion of legal validity; the distinction between duty-imposing and power-conferring rules; the internal and external aspects of rules; and judicial discretion. In fact, much of the analytical material contained in chapters I–VII of *The Concept of Law* could be said to constitute Hart's nucleic expository theory in the sense of the present discussion.

exists, is a law, though we happen to dislike it, or though it vary from the text, by which we regulate our approbation and disapprobation". See John Austin, *The Province of Jurisprudence Determined* (Hackett Publishing Co. Inc., Indianapolis, 1998), 184 (Lecture V).

[7] *CL*, 302.

[8] See Stanley L Paulson's Introduction to Hans Kelsen, *Introduction to the Problems of Legal Theory* (Clarendon Press, Oxford, 1992) (*PTL*) xxiv and n. 17. See also Ronald Dworkin, *Taking Rights Seriously* (Fifth Impression) (Gerald Duckworth & Co. Ltd., 1977), 17. Dworkin outlines (legal) positivism's "few central and organizing propositions".

The concept of Law: Hart's nucleic expository theory

It has been recognised that at mid-century, jurisprudence as taught at universities in Britain had reached a critical phase in which the primary emphasis of academic law was expository and analytical in a narrow sense rather than philosophical or critical.[9] The attention of legal academics was securely focused on issues such as the interpretation and analysis of existing legal doctrine and precedent. At the time there was no place for attempting to locate law within a wider frame of reference presented by disciplines such as sociology, political theory or economics. Hart's unique achievement was to effect a gradual yet radical change in the way law—and the academic study of law: jurisprudence—was perceived in Britain and the English-speaking world. Even among Hart's severest critics there is recognition that *The Concept of Law* and Hart's other writings rank among the most profound and influential contributions to legal philosophy in the twentieth century.

Hart's General Approach

We have seen that in *The Concept of Law* Hart formulated and developed an approach to legal theory applying the ordinary language philosophy of J L Austin. Hart's inaugural lecture, "Definition and Theory in Jurisprudence", was a portent of this new approach.[10] In his lecture Hart suggested that fundamental legal notions could be elucidated by methods properly adapted to their special character. Hart opposed the quest for definitions of expressions such as "law", "state", "right" and "corporation". It is futile, he claimed, to search for a counterpart to such notions in the "real world" or to apply the method of definition *per genus et differentiam*: positioning the notion within a class or generic group of which it is perceived to be a member, then listing the features which

---

[9] See Twining, above at n. 4, at 559. See also E Bodenheimer, "Modern Analytical Jurisprudence and the Limits of Its Usefulness" (1955–56) 104 *University of Pennsylvania Law Review* 1080; H L A Hart, "Analytical Jurisprudence in Mid-Twentieth Century: A Reply to Professor Bodenheimer" (1957) 105 *University of Pennsylvania Law Review* 953.

[10] H L A Hart, "Definition and Theory in Jurisprudence" (1954) 70 *Law Quarterly Review* 37. See esp. 41.

differentiate it from other notions within the same class. A definition of "law" as a member of the general class of rules of behaviour was rejected in *The Concept of Law* because the concept of "rule" is itself as problematic as that of "law", in Hart's view.[11]

Hart argued that it makes no sense to abstract legal expressions from their normal context. The meaning of fundamental legal notions could be elucidated if incorporated in sentences in which they play their characteristic or typical role. The conditions under which those sentences are true may then be identified. As a *practical* proposition, then, meaning was to be discovered by careful analysis of the use of fundamental notions in typical legal discourse. In a shift of emphasis, *The Concept of Law* widened this approach to a consideration of the *social* context of typical legal discourse. So, for example, in discussing the use of the imperative linguistic form in the context of Austin's command theory, Hart considers at least two social situations in which that form is typically used: coercive orders issued by a gunman to a bank clerk and the use of commands in a military setting. The application of the ordinary language philosophical method is clearly evident throughout *The Concept of Law*. At every opportunity Hart situates the language of law—e.g., expressions such as "duty", "obedience", "habit", and so on—in particular social contexts and clarifies the sense and significance of the selected expressions in those contexts. The problem of whether these or other scenarios genuinely constitute settings for "typical" legal discourse was not addressed. Hart neither specified criteria of typicality, nor sought to justify his selection of particular discourse-laden scenarios.

Hart's Three Recurrent Issues

As previously noted, Hart's overall aim was to address three issues that had recurred in the speculations of legal philosophers and others who had been concerned to understand the idea of law. As an approach to elucidating "law", definition was rejected since there was nothing, in Hart's view, sufficiently concise to provide a satisfactory answer to the question "what is law?".[12] This led Hart to the three recurrent issues underlying that question. In Hart's view

[11] *CL*, 15.
[12] Ibid., 16.

these issues were too different to be capable of a mode of resolution that entails mere definition.

Recast as questions, the three recurrent issues are:

1. How do law and legal obligation differ from, and how are they related to, orders backed by threats?
2. How does law differ from, and how is it related to, moral obligation?
3. What are rules and to what extent is law an affair of rules?[13]

In attempting to address each of these questions in turn Hart sets out "to advance legal theory by providing an improved analysis of the distinctive structure of a municipal legal system and a better understanding of the resemblances and differences between law, coercion and morality as types of social phenomena".[14] The overall result of Hart's approach is a tapestry of clarifications, distinctions, necessary and sufficient truth conditions, dissolved "perplexities" and resolved confusions. This builds to a grander narrative as Hart modulates imperceptibly towards a specific view of law which is, in fact, curiously *definitional*. Hart may not have proffered a single, definitive word formulation to serve as a definition of municipal law, but it is clear that for Hart the answer to the question "what is law?" is the totality of the distinctions and clarifications which he makes. That is not to say that the means by which Hart arrives at his specific concept of law is unimportant. Nonetheless, in the final analysis it is possible to reconstruct Hart's concept of law if not in terms of a concise simple definition then as a series of interdependent propositions which—a sceptic might observe—unravel to something approximating a definition of a specific type of law within a specific political ethos: western, liberal, rule of law.[15]

---

[13] CL, 6–17.

[14] Ibid., 17.

[15] Donald Galloway notes that, despite Hart's stated position regarding the use of definition, the *end result* of Hart's theorising is actually definition. See "The Axiology of Analytical Jurisprudence: A Study of the Underlying Sociological Assumptions and Ideological Predilections", in Thomas W Bechtler (ed.), *Law in a Social Context: Liber Amicorum Honouring Professor Lon L. Fuller* (Kluwer, The Netherlands, 1978), 49 at 78–9.

For instance, Hart stresses that individual laws are framed in general terms.[16] The notion of equal subjection of officials and citizenry to law is also a feature of Hart's model of law.[17] The non-retrospectivity of laws is recognised as a required feature of law.[18] For Hart, law is elementally a "means of social control".[19] Hart's paradigmatic "modern municipal legal system" is expressed in the separation of powers model of governance which entails the division of governmental functions into judicial, executive and legislative functions. Although Hart has little to say in *The Concept of Law* about the interplay between electorate and legislature, his concept of a modern municipal legal system presupposes the notion of a centrally organised, democratically elected representative legislature.[20] Other features that can be assigned to Hart's conception of law flow from his notion of law operating within an institutional context, in which officials and special agencies have administrative and enforcement roles.[21] Hart's conception of law thus incorporates a faintly Weberian notion of governance through centrally organised, rational, bureaucratic structures of official roles and functions.[22]

Ironically, one of the consequences of Hart's eschewal of definition is the requirement *nonetheless* to reconstruct a working conception of law—in effect, a definition—from discrete *indicia* scattered randomly throughout *The Concept of Law*. To that extent it seems clear that Hart fails to establish convincingly that definition, or for that matter preliminary boundary-drawing, can be dispensed with. The reconstruction exercise simply renders more tortuous the task of discerning Hart's particular conception of law. Yet the rationale behind Hart's opposition to the use of definition seems sound in principle in cases where *only* a definition of law is offered in response to the macro-question "what is law?". Theory, not

---

[16] *CL*, 21–2.
[17] Ibid., generally ch. 2.
[18] Ibid., 276.
[19] See, for example ibid., 40, 90, 91.
[20] Ibid., 74.
[21] Ibid., 93.
[22] See Galloway, above at n. 15, at 82. Galloway stresses that Hart's paradigm for law is the legal order of a modern western democracy, distinguished by its alleged adherence to the rule of law. See also Max Weber, *Economy and Society. An Outline of Interpretive Sociology* (Bedminster Press Inc., New York, 1968) (*ES*), 217–226.

definition, is the appropriate response. There are obviously cases, though, where definition in the context of theory is a useful tool to fix ideas as a preliminary context for discussion: "I propose to discuss X by which for present purposes I mean . . .". Any particular aspects of X, idiosyncrasies, problematical areas, or exceptions from the general definition can be clarified in the course of the unfolding discussion. Subsidiary definitions can also be used to facilitate the flow of an argument or to set the boundaries of peripheral concepts that are useful to the theory. In Weber's *Economy and Society*[23] numerous relatively minor "building-block" definitions are used, widely and effectively, to contribute to a more encompassing totality.[24]

Law as Primary and Secondary Rules

For Hart, "law" in the sense of the municipal law of a modern state comprises a system which combines two distinct types of legal rules: *primary rules* and *secondary rules*. The union of primary and secondary rules is a central notion in Hart's jurisprudence and is, in a sense, the most "definitional" proposition in *The Concept of Law*. It is "the heart of a legal system" and "a most powerful tool for the analysis of much that has puzzled both the jurist and the political theorist".[25]

Primary rules principally (and, because this is not made clear, *may*, for Hart, exhaustively) comprise rules of obligation. It is not entirely certain from Hart's analysis whether facilitative power-conferring rules—such as those enabling the creation of a valid will or the formation of a contract—can be classified as primary rules. There seems no reason in principle for excluding those rules from the classification "primary", other than that they function in effect as rules of change which are secondary in terms of Hart's scheme. In general, primary rules impose legal duties and thereby render behaviour non-optional. A criminal statute is characteristic of a complex of rules of the primary kind. Such a statute defines certain kinds of conduct as something which is to be done or avoided by individuals to whom the statute applies, irrespective of the wishes of those individuals. Punishments or "sanctions" attach to criminal

---

[23] Above at n. 22..
[24] See, for example, ibid., 24–6, 29–31, 34–6, 53–4.
[25] *CL*, 98.

laws. Hart notes a strong analogy between criminal law and the model of law as the sovereign's coercive orders attributed by Hart to John Austin. Civil laws which provide individuals with compensation for civil wrongs—torts or delicts—perpetrated on those individuals by others are a further example of laws in the primary sense. A social structure of primary rules of obligation might be organised on the basis of rules restricting the free use of violence, theft and deception, and rules imposing duties to perform services or make contributions to the common life.

Hart describes secondary rules as "parasitic upon" primary rules. While primary rules are concerned with actions which individuals must or must not do, secondary rules are concerned with the primary rules themselves. According to Hart, secondary rules "specify the ways in which the primary rules may be conclusively ascertained, introduced, eliminated, varied, and the fact of their violation conclusively determined".[26] Hart establishes a tripartite classification of secondary rules: the *rule (or rules) of recognition, rules of change* and *rules of adjudication.*

Hart presents the rule of recognition as the "remedy" introduced to address the uncertainty that might prevail in an imaginary primitive community whose only mode of social control is rules of obligation which equate to rules in the primary sense. In such a "pre-legal" community, according to Hart, rules are not systematically ordered and unified; rather, they comprise separate and discrete standards of behaviour. In Hart's hypothetical community there is no authoritative procedure for identifying the social rules which govern the lives of its inhabitants. The rule of recognition specifies some feature possession of which by a rule conclusively indicates that it is a rule of the group to be supported by the social pressure it exerts. In a developed legal system, complex *rules* of recognition may be embodied in an authoritative text which organises the rules in order of superiority to avoid internal inconsistency. In Hart's view the notion of the systemic nature of law is accountable to the rule of recognition: "for the rules are now not just a discrete unconnected set but are, in a simple way, unified".[27]

[26] Ibid., 94. See also 81.
[27] Ibid., 95.

Law as a Social Institution

but here
(i) feature of the rule
(ii) feature of how the rule came about "pedigree"

The idea of legal validity derives from the rule of recognition. A legal rule is a valid rule of a given legal system if it satisfies criteria of identification—tests of "pedigree", as Dworkin describes it[28]—specified in the rule of recognition. The rule of recognition, along with other secondary rules, must be accepted by officials from the *internal point of view* (as discussed later in this chapter) as a public common standard of official behaviour in recognising primary rules by reference to appropriate identifying criteria.

Rules of change are presented as the "remedy" for the static quality of a regime of primary rules existing in an imaginary primitive community. Now significantly, Hart does not explore the possibility of a lawmaking *structure* being introduced. While this may be a necessary concomitant of the introduction of the relevant rules, it nonetheless serves to accentuate that for Hart a legal system is characterised as a system of *rules*.[29] On another view a legal system could be said to combine legal norms *and organised institutional social structures*: in other words, a symbiosis of the interdependent elements of normativity and institutionality.

but what are these?

but some processes act + that isn't a rule of change

In its simplest form, a rule of change is power-conferring. It empowers an individual or body to introduce new primary rules and eliminate old ones. In a developed, complex society legislation is enacted and repealed under the authority of rules of change. The rules may be simple or complex and may confer unrestricted or limited powers. Rules of change define procedures to be followed in enacting legislation and identify the persons who are to participate in the legislative process.

In Hart's "pre-legal" community the only mechanism for the "enforcement" of the simple regime of primary rules is diffuse social pressure. Hart regards this as inefficient: disputes will occur

---

[28] See Ronald Dworkin, *Taking Rights Seriously* (Fifth Impression) (Gerald Duckworth & Co. Ltd., 1977), 17.

[29] Hart comes to see the existence of "effective law-applying and law-enforcing" *agencies* in a significantly later essay as a "feature of crucial importance in the development of a [legal] system" which is "missing" from a version of the "pre-legal" society which Hart describes in the course of the same essay. See "Commands and Authoritative Legal Reasons", in Hart, *Essays on Bentham: Studies in Jurisprudence and Political Theory* (Clarendon Press, Oxford, 1982), 257–8. There, Hart also discusses "institutionalization". Regrettably, Hart does not give similar prominence to institutional structures in *The Concept of Law* (nor even in the *Postscript* to *The Concept of Law*).

and will continue interminably if there is no agency specially empowered to ascertain, finally and authoritatively, the fact of violation. A further weakness is the lack of an agency to administer punishments for violations of the rules. To address these deficiencies, again *rules* are required, not institutional structures, though again that may be implicit in Hart's analysis. Secondary rules of adjudication are the "remedy" for inefficiency. Rules of adjudication empower individuals to make authoritative determinations as to whether there have been infringements of primary rules. Rules of adjudication identify persons who are to adjudicate and define procedures to be followed in making authoritative determinations. According to Hart, they "define a group of important legal concepts: . . . the concepts of judge or court, jurisdiction and judgment".[30] It is interesting to note Hart's use of the expressions "define" and "legal concepts" in this context. There is almost a sense in which rules of adjudication, for Hart, *call into existence* courts and court officials; and when courts and officials exist they do so only as "concepts", not as human beings. Thus, only "rules" seem to exist. Rules, not individuals, become "protagonists", as Donald Galloway has observed.[31] This de-personalising of the institutional face of the legal system and attendant emphasis on rules— as opposed to persons: social actors—is critically examined in chapter 4 below.

Secondary rules are interconnected in various ways. Rules of recognition incorporate references to identifying features of the legal rules, or legislation, created under powers conferred by rules of change. Rules of adjudication contain references to the rules of recognition which in turn identify what is to count as valid primary rules of the system in respect of which authoritative determinations are to be made. The rule of adjudication which confers jurisdiction, therefore, is a rule of recognition which identifies primary rules.

Thus, the union of primary and secondary rules is the core of what is described here as Hart's nucleic expository theory. This combination of types of rules may not amount to a "definition" of law in any accepted sense, but is one of the key defining notions of Hart's jurisprudence. Hart's tripartite classification of secondary

---

[30] *CL*, 97.
[31] Galloway, above at n. 15, at 84.

rules, as I have previously mentioned, corresponds approximately to elements of the doctrine of the separation of legislative, judicial and executive powers developed by Locke and Montesquieu and accepted as a constitutional "norm" for democratic systems of government in many parts of the world.[32] Rules of adjudication and recognition embody functions of the judiciary, while rules of change structure the legislative function. In his typology of secondary rules, Hart does not specifically address the executive function of government, although it is possibly buried in an extended notion of rules of adjudication: the carrying-out of the orders of a judge by court officials being seen as a practical "extension" of adjudication. Furthermore, the executive arm of government inevitably uses criteria, if not rules, of recognition in identifying laws which it is to enforce through executive action. It is arguable, then, that although *rules of executive action* may have been passed over in Hart's classification of secondary rules, the spectre of such rules can be extrapolated from rules of adjudication and recognition. After all, when he first discusses rules of adjudication, Hart mentions the problem in a "pre-legal" society associated with "the fact that punishments for violations of the rules, and other forms of social pressure involving physical effort or the use of force, are not administered by a special agency but are left to the individuals affected or to the group at large".[33] In general, rules of administrative law and rules dealing with the enforcement of orders and decisions of courts could be the subject of a further category of rules of executive action added to Hart's typology of secondary rules.

So far as the model of "pre-legal" societies is concerned, it is probable that Hart not only underestimates the likely ingenuity and

---

[32] See, for example, Montesquieu, *L'Esprit des Lois* (*The Spirit of the Laws*) (1748) (Collier Macmillan, London, 1949); John Locke, *Two Treatises of Government*, (Cambridge University Press, Cambridge, 1988) (1993 reprint), 117–21 and 364 *et seq*. See also Alfred Cobban, *Rousseau and the Modern State* (George Allen & Unwin Ltd., London, 2nd ed. 1964), 81 *et seq*.

[33] *CL*, 93. Rolf Sartorius comments on this "apparent gap" in Hart's theory. He suggests that the gap may be filled by further secondary rules that confer on judges the exclusive power to direct the application of penalties by other officials. Sartorius suggests that these rules might have been called "rules of enforcement". See Rolf Sartorius, "Positivism and Legal Authority", in Ruth Gavison (ed.), *Issues in Contemporary Legal Philosophy: The Influence of H.L.A. Hart* (Clarendon Press, Oxford, 1987) (1992 paperback reprint), 45.

resourcefulness of societies which could conceivably fit this description but he surely also misdescribes the "step" from the "pre-legal" to the "legal".[34] It is not a necessary—in the sense of ineluctable—development in the context of a hypothetical progression from "pre-legal" to "legal" modes of social control that the features embodied in the doctrine of the separation of powers should accompany such a development. The doctrine was an innovation in the history of western political organisation and theory. The development towards a separation of powers model cannot be said to represent an inevitable step either in the natural order of things or in the historical evolution of events. Nor can features of the rule of law model of government implicit in Hart's analysis—such as the equal subjection of officials as well as citizens to law and the generality or "equivalent applicability" of law to all classes of citizens—be considered an inevitable step.

If the primary–secondary dichotomy of rules represented all that there was to Hart's nucleic expository theory—attempting, as it did, to give an account of a modern municipal legal system—then that alone would have marked an inventive departure from the theories _well, Hohfeld_ of law that pre-dated _The Concept of Law._ There is, of course, somewhat more to Hart's notion of municipal law. In particular, against the background of a critique of a version of Austinian jurisprudence which Hart sets up as a target of analytical enquiry, Hart outlines and elucidates two further key distinctions:

1. the distinction between duty-imposing and power-conferring rules; and
2. the distinction between internal and external aspects of rules (and corresponding internal and external points of view).

It is important to note Hart's acknowledgement in _The Concept of Law_ that the "Austinian" model which he "reconstructs" in order to criticise—essentially that of law as coercive orders of the sovereign habitually obeyed by the population at large—is, according to Hart, "in substance, the same as Austin's doctrine but probably diverges from it at certain points".[35] Hart states his principal

---

[34] See Martin Krygier, "_The Concept of Law_ and Social Theory" (1982) 2 _Oxford Journal of Legal Studies_ 155, 171–8.

[35] _CL_, 18.

concern not to be with Austin but with the credentials of a certain type of theory which has proved attractive despite its perceived defects. His aim therefore is to present a strengthened, clear and consistent version of "Austinian" theory as a focus of critical attention. Even in instances where Austin merely offered "hints" as to his position, Hart claims to develop that position in order that the doctrine which he criticises is formulated in its strongest form. Hart has been criticised for distorting Austin's theory and perpetuating considerable misinterpretation of Austinian jurisprudence.[36] Yet *in a qualified sense* many of the clarifications and insights generated by Hart's approach and any resulting advances in legal understanding can be evaluated independently of the question of whether Hart gave a fair and accurate account of Austin's work. Against the notion of law as the commands or coercive orders of a sovereign, Hart makes a series of observations which serve to clarify the nature of law as constituted by *rules*. Legal rules may *include* imperative forms analogous to "commands", such as penal statutes, but they are not exhaustively reducible to such forms.

Hart's attack on the notion of law as coercive orders initially centres on the impracticability of supporting the number of officials necessary to inform each and every member of a given community of the standards of behaviour to which they must conform. Legal control is achieved through laws which are general rather than individual in this sense. It does not involve a vast multiplicity of individualised situational commands. Moreover, even if a criminal statute superficially resembles a coercive order it differs from such an order in applying to those who enacted it. The continuity of laws through successive changes of sovereign, which in the parallel context of a modern legal system equates to continuity of legislative authority, is not satisfactorily explained by the notion of a commanding sovereign. It is, rather, explained by the presence of *rules* of succession or rules establishing the continuity of legislative power.

Handwritten margin notes: "technical argument"; "'order' is wrong b... 1. law is general 2. law applies to those who issue it"

Duty-imposing and Power-conferring Rules

Another attack by Hart on the idea of law as coercive orders arises in the context of the distinction between duty-imposing and power-

[36] See, generally, Robert N Moles, *Definition and Rule in Legal Theory: A Reassessment of H.L.A. Hart and the Positivist Tradition* (Basil Blackwell Ltd., Oxford, 1987).

conferring laws. This distinction is by no means Hart's innovation, nor would Hart have claimed it to be so. The provenance of the distinction is more difficult to trace. In the twentieth century, W N Hohfeld's ground-breaking treatise, *Fundamental Legal Conceptions as Applied in Judicial Reasoning*,[37] identifies what are, in effect, the most fundamental and irreducible legal concepts. Hohfeld formulates an eight-term relational configuration of legal concepts. The legal relationships, or *jural relations*, can be divided into two families of four terms which correspond loosely to Hart's distinction between duty-imposing and power-conferring legal rules. In the duty-imposing family of relationships, right and duty in the "strict" sense are correlatives, while in the power-conferring family, power and liability are correlatives. Each set of correlatives has opposites. But while Hohfeld was the first to configure legal relationships in this way, the essential difference between legal rights in the "strict" sense and legal powers had been recognised previously and—as Hart in a later work readily acknowledges—by writers including Bentham.[38]

Hart argues that certain power-conferring or facilitative laws— such as those defining the ways in which contracts are validly constituted or marriages solemnised—perform a different social function from criminal laws and cannot, without absurdity, be construed as orders backed by the sanction of punishment. To that extent, such legal rules are not readily explained in terms of a model of law as coercive orders. Hart's category of facilitative laws is doubtless wider than Hohfeld's more abstract category of correlatively structured power↔liability legal relationships in that facilitative laws are made up of complex *structures* of interrelated legal rules. Such juridical structures are the basis for what Neil MacCormick has described as "institutions" of the law.[39] In any event, Hart includes among power-conferring legal rules the more

[handwritten margin note: ok, but are these inc. in secondary rules, then?]

[37] Wesley Newcomb Hohfeld, *Fundamental Legal Conceptions as Applied in Judicial Reasoning* (Yale University Press, 4th Printing, 1966).

[38] H L A Hart, *Essays on Bentham: Studies in Jurisprudence and Political Theory* (Clarendon Press, Oxford, 1982), 195–6.

[39] See, generally, Neil MacCormick's inaugural lecture, "Law as Institutional Fact", reprinted as ch. II in Neil MacCormick and Ota Weinberger, *An Institutional Theory of Law: New Approaches to Legal Positivism* (D Reidel Publishing Co., Dordrecht, Holland, 1986), 49 *et seq.*; previously published in (1974) 90 *Law Quarterly Review* 102.

abstract Hohfeldian legal powers to adjudicate or legislate (public powers) and to create or vary legal relations (private powers). In an extended series of arguments, Hart considers the conceptual distortion that results if the nullity effect of non-compliance with power-conferring laws is perceived as a "sanction", or if power-conferring laws are recast in terms of fragments of duty-imposing laws. Distortion, in Hart's view, is the price to be paid for the uniformity of treating duty-imposing and power-conferring laws as essentially "the same thing", namely coercive orders.

Internal and External Aspect of Rules

The focal point of Hart's assault on the "Austinian" model of law is the distinction which he draws between internal and external aspects of rules. This is perhaps one of the most fundamental distinctions in *The Concept of Law*, and in different ways is crucial in the overall context of Hart's theory. It is significant in any event because it marks the beginnings of a tendency towards mainstream social theory: in particular towards Weber's method of interpretive understanding (*Verstehen*) which I briefly discussed in chapter 2.[40] In a rudimentary way, Hart's distinction also touches upon Weber's method of causal explanation in terms of the inferences which may be drawn from externally observable regularities of human behaviour. The wider significance of Hart's internal–external metaphor was to introduce to analytical jurisprudence the rudiments of an approach which has come to be known as *legal hermeneutics*.[41] Law is to be seen as a normative system: a network of social rules—of which law is a sub-type—which guide human action from an internal point of view and establish standards of social conduct.

It is clear at the outset that the distinction between the two aspects of rules, and their corresponding viewpoints, suffers from functional ambiguity and analytical confusion. What role does the distinction play: is it purely methodological, or are there underlying substantive issues? On the assumption that there *are* substantive

[40] Roger Cotterrell, in *The Politics of Jurisprudence: A Critical Introduction to Legal Philosophy* (Butterworths, London and Edinburgh, 1989), 94–6, refers to this tendency in Hart as "sociological drift".

[41] See Neil MacCormick, *H.L.A. Hart* (Edward Arnold (Publishers) Ltd., London, 1981), 32. See also Gregory Leyh (ed.), *Legal Hermeneutics: History, Theory and Practice* (University of California Press, Berkeley and Los Angeles, 1992).

issues, how are those issues to be structured and prioritised as among different classes of persons? For instance, to what extent is Hart's portrayal of internal attitudes to rules—specifically, as between officials working "within" the system and "everyone else"—tenable? It is clear that methodological and substantive issues are conflated in the course of Hart's presentation whilst substantive issues are less than satisfactorily portrayed. As an initial task, then, it is useful to attempt a sympathetic reconstruction of the external and internal aspects of rules to allow the import and significance of that distinction to be properly conveyed. To that end I shall follow Neil MacCormick's account of Hart's position.[42]

If we initially take the view that Hart is making a *methodological* point—a point about how knowledge of the legal world is obtained—an appropriate starting point is the external aspect of rules and point of view as Hart depicts them. Hart frequently uses the viewpoint of an "external observer" as a heuristic device to characterise particular ways of viewing law, or law-affected behaviour, or human behaviour in general. Where the external observer is seen to adopt an extreme empiricist approach to the observation of human behaviour he or she merely notes external regularities or repeated patterns of behaviour without in any sense engaging with the mind—the motivations, impulses or mental content—of the subjects observed. Hart gives the example of traffic coming to a halt at red traffic lights. All that is observed is that there is merely a high probability that traffic will stop. Adopting Weberian terminology, one "event" (traffic halting) is seen to follow another "event" (the light turning to red) in a relationship of cause and effect: the red traffic light is observed to "cause" traffic to halt. In no sense, however, is the relationship perceived as rule-governed from the point of view of the vehicle driver. Nor is there any attempt by the observer to enter, or attain an insight, into the mental processes of any specific driver. On this view the red traffic light is not accounted "causative" of a response on the part of the driver which impels an act—halting the vehicle—in compliance with a legal rule requiring this response. Hart refers to this perspective as the "extreme external point of view".[43] Unlike the non-extreme external point of view

---

[42] See MacCormick, above at n. 41, at 29 *et seq.*

[43] *CL,* 89.

considered below, the extreme external point of view is not especially significant in methodological terms, although it perhaps bears a superficial similarity to aspects of the causal dimension of Weber's methodology.

Hart also acknowledges a "weaker"—or less "hard empiricist"—version of the external observer's viewpoint: a non-extreme external point of view. As MacCormick suggests, it is an unsatisfactory feature of Hart's account that he passes too lightly over this viewpoint.[44] For, if sufficiently developed, it could have equated to the classic viewpoint of the observer acting in the role of social scientific investigator. In the legal theory setting, such an observer could take on the mantle of—to use MacCormick's expression—"Hartian legal theorist". Here the observer *does* make the linkage between patterns of behaviour—in the sense of externally observable regularities of human conduct—and the use of social (legal) rules as a reference point for the orientation of that behaviour. In other words, the observer, in making the connection between rules and rule-compliant behaviour, seeks to understand the rule-compliant behaviour from the (internal) point of view of the actor. But as MacCormick notes, the observer must restrict himself to describing "legal rules as they are held from the internal point of view regardless of any commitment he himself has for or against these rules in their internal aspect". In other words the observer—pursuant, possibly, to a methodological principle of scientific objectivity—approaches the object of enquiry with detachment and disinterestedness. MacCormick describes this non-extreme external point of view as the "hermeneutic" point of view and commends it as "the central methodological insight of Hart's analytical jurisprudence".[45] If Hart had delineated the viewpoint of the scientific investigator more coherently and fashioned its theoretical consequences as a methodological *standard* for legal theory he would arguably have been less vulnerable to the accusations of sociological isolationism briefly mentioned in chapter 1.

[44] See MacCormick, above at n. 41, at 37. Gerald J Postema also examines some aspects of Hart's position on "detached judgements" in the context of what he calls "observer theory", in "The Normativity of Law", in Ruth Gavison (ed.), *Issues in Contemporary Legal Philosophy: The Influence of H.L.A. Hart* (Clarendon Press, Oxford, 1987) (1992 paperback reprint), 81 *et seq*. In particular, see 83–93.

[45] See MacCormick, above at n. 41, at 38.

With the benefit of MacCormick's reading of Hart, the non-extreme external point of view—embodied in the position of the investigative observer—is seen to be defined in terms of the observer's interest in certain external regularities or patterns of behaviour. In addition, the observer has a detached interest in the behaviour of the observed subject seen from the subject's internal point of view as that is perceived, however imperfectly, by the observer. From that point of view the behaviour may be found to constitute rule-compliant behaviour.

Hart occasionally uses versions of the external aspect of rules to make a substantive point designed to accentuate features of the internal aspect of rules. The external point of view in this sense is held by individuals who are *members* of the hypothetical social group whose behaviour and attitudes Hart speculatively discusses. Such group members reject the rules of the group and see them merely as a basis for causal predictions that punishment will follow violation of the rules. To that extent an extreme external point of view which approximates to that of an observer is reproduced in the lives of those group members who reject the group's rules. But, as Hart argues, this point of view fails to reproduce from an *internal* point of view the way:[46]

> "in which the rules function as rules in the lives of those who normally are the majority of society. These are the officials, lawyers, or private persons who use them, in one situation after another, as guides to the conduct of social life, as the basis for claims, demands, admissions, criticism, or punishment . . .".

What, then, *is* the internal point of view as Hart characterises it? The emphasis of the discussion is focused at a *substantive* rather than methodological level: at the level of the observed subject who is said to possess an internal point of view. Again, we follow Neil MacCormick's account of Hart's position.

The notion of the internal aspect of rules first arises in the context of Hart's discussion of behaviour which he claims to be characteristic of the citizenry in the "Austinian" model of coercive orders—the habitual obedience rendered by the citizenry to the sovereign. Hart argues that laws are *social rules*. Therefore behaviour

[46] *CL*, 90.

55

complying with laws is to be characterised in the same terms as behaviour complying with social rules.[47] According to Hart, social rules are not maintained in existence by virtue of a habit of obedience. A habit as Hart characterises it—or, perhaps more accurately, caricatures it—is a form of behaviour which is unthinking: almost automaton-like and certainly unlike the attitude characteristic of the internal attitude as Hart portrays this. The important issue here, however, is not the plausibility of Hart's characterisation of habitual behaviour; it is his characterisation of behaviour in accordance with social rules. As Hart observes:[48]

> "[I]f a social rule is to exist some at least must look upon the behaviour in question as a general standard to be followed by the group as a whole. A social rule has an 'internal' aspect, in addition to the external aspect which it shares with a social habit and which consists in the regular uniform behaviour which an observer could record."

Hart develops this further in a key passage:[49]

> "What is necessary [for the existence of 'binding' social rules] is that there should be a critical reflective attitude to certain patterns of behaviour as a common standard, and that this should display itself in criticism (including self-criticism), demands for conformity, and in acknowledgements that such criticism and demands are justified, all of which find their characteristic expression in the normative terminology of 'ought', 'must', and 'should', 'right' and 'wrong'."

The existence of a critical reflective attitude is the essence of Hart's notion of the internal aspect of social rules and, in so far as laws are social rules, it is a central component of the internal aspect of legal rules as Hart depicts this. At many places in *The Concept of Law*, Hart additionally presents the internal aspect of rules as an attitude of "acceptance" of rules, but he does not usefully elaborate upon this notion.

MacCormick identifies two main components of the critical reflective attitude: a cognitive element and a volitional element. The cognitive element—the "reflective" component of Hart's formula-

[47] In the *Postscript* to *The Concept of Law*, Hart seemingly modifies his position such as to exclude "enacted laws" from the category of laws that could be regarded as Hartian "social rules". For further discussion, see chapter 6 below.

[48] *CL*, 56.

[49] Ibid., 57.

tion—covers the human capacity to conceive behaviour in abstract terms and to correlate (for instance in causal terms) one event with another: drivers halting vehicles at red traffic lights. It also encompasses the ability to evaluate behaviour in terms of (as the case may be) conforming, not conforming, or being irrelevant, to a perceived general pattern of behaviour. The volitional element—the "critical" component of Hart's formulation—entails some desire or preference that the act, or abstention from acting, be done when certain envisaged circumstances obtain. It may be that such a preference holds only for so long as there continues to be a *shared* preference that a particular mode or pattern of behaviour be adhered to within an identifiable social group. Although there may also be an *emotional* element so far as distinguishable from the volitional—a "mere matter of 'feelings'" as Hart puts it—this is, in fact, peripheral to Hart's analysis. A "binding social rule" in Hart's sense may engender psychological experiences of "restriction" or "compulsion" which are neither necessary nor sufficient for the existence of such a rule. While MacCormick considers the volitional element to be more important than affective or emotional attitudes, he nonetheless considers it to be an error to sever the emotional element entirely from the volitional element in any consideration of social rules.[50] The internal aspect of rules is thus understandable in terms of the attitude of those who act upon a preference for a particular mode or pattern of behaviour to be adhered to by themselves and others. This preference is manifested in "acceptance" of the rules, criticism, demands for conformity and the use of normative language. The relevant criticism and demands are furthermore "justified" or legitimate.

Hart's internal–external distinction has a special role in the legal setting. For, according to Hart, there are two minimum conditions necessary and sufficient for the existence of a legal system. First, the primary rules of the system must be generally obeyed by private citizens who in a "healthy society" will often accept these rules as common standards of behaviour from the internal point of view. These legal rules, in other words, function in the same way as "social rules" in Hart's sense. Secondly, the rules of recognition, adjudication and change—the secondary rules of the system—must

[50] MacCormick, above at n. 41, at 34.

be effectively accepted as common standards of official behaviour by officials and used by those officials to appraise critically their own and each other's deviations as lapses. In particular, the rule of recognition "must be regarded from the internal point of view as a public, common standard of correct judicial decision, and not as something which each judge merely obeys for his part only".[51]

The Open-Textured Nature of Rules—Judicial Discretion

Hart's linguistic philosophical outlook—in particular his reflections on the nature of language—and his positioning of legal rules at the centre of the legal universe combine in a curious way to define a key aspect of the judicial role: judicial discretion. The starting point for Hart is a conception of the legal rule as an essentially linguistic form. As language, according to Hart, has an open-textured nature—a degree of indeterminacy that makes it liable to interpretation—so also do legal rules. This holds whether the rules in question are judge-made or in the nature of legislation:[52]

> "Whichever device, precedent or legislation, is chosen for the communication of standards of behaviour, these, however smoothly they work over the great mass of ordinary cases, will, at some point where their application is in question prove indeterminate; they will have what has been termed an *open texture*." benign : say indeterminate.

In addition, the characteristic *generality* of legal rules as an intrinsic feature necessitates interpretive choices to be made at the level of rule application. This generality, in Hart's view, has a twofold origin: (i) in our relative ignorance of fact and (ii) in our relative indeterminacy of aim. If the world comprised a finite number of features, and if these, together with all possible combinations of features, were known, detailed provision could be made in advance for every possibility. There would be a legal rule to cover every eventuality and the relevant rule could be mechanically applied as and when that eventuality arose. That is not the way of the world, however. To that extent we are, relatively speaking, ignorant of the factual circumstances that could arise in the future. The inability to anticipate circumstances in advance brings with it the second

the claim that circumstances are new.

---

[51] *CL*, 116.
[52] Ibid., 127–8.

factor necessitating generality: an indeterminacy of aim. A general rule is usually framed in a context in which clear cases requiring to be subsumed by the rule *are* known in advance, whilst unanticipated or less clear cases—which might just come within the spirit of the "mischief" which the rule is designed to address (e.g., preservation of public order)—are not known. As it may be desirable for unanticipated cases of a certain kind to be covered by the rule *if they should happen to occur in the future,* the relative indeterminacy of aim which is an essential incident of the rule may be regarded as a positive advantage.[53]

Hart points out that all systems compromise between the need to attain *certainty* where legal rules can safely be applied by private individuals to themselves without official guidance, and the need to leave matters *open* for settlement in an official forum in the concrete case as and when it arises. A legal culture which adopts a formalistic approach narrows the parameters of judicial interpretation and thus sacrifices too much to certainty. The result, according to Hart, may be a failure to respond to similarities or differences between cases which only surface when the issues are seen in the light of social aims. In other systems, on the other hand, too much may be left open to perpetual revision or reconsideration.[54]

Against this background, Hart concludes that in every legal system a large and significant field is left open for the exercise of discretion by courts and officials in making initially vague standards of behaviour concrete and precise, in resolving uncertainties in statutory law and in qualifying and developing rules of law broadly conveyed in judicial decisions. Hart's "point of arrival"—that there is a field for the exercise of discretion by courts and officials necessitated by the structure of language and of legal rules—is similar to Kelsen's view that there is a range of discretion corresponding to intended and unintended indeterminacy of legal norms. Kelsen's development of this position led him to a view of the legal norm as a "frame" according to which an act of legal "interpretation" involves discovery of the frame that the norm to be applied represents and the cognition within that frame of various possibilities for

---

[53] Generally, ibid., 128–9.
[54] Ibid., 130.

application.[55] Like Kelsen, Hart also recognises that interpreting a statute may not necessarily lead to a single decision as the only correct decision but to a number of possible decisions from which a *choice* is made as to the most appropriate decision for the particular situation in hand.

Three Recurrent Issues—Hart's Response

A general public attitude of acceptance of primary rules, combined with a particular official attitude of acceptance of secondary rules—reflecting the "union" of primary and secondary rules—is the nucleus of Hart's expository jurisprudence. This configuration—primary rules harnessed to the citizenry and their internalised general acceptance of those rules; and secondary rules harnessed to public officials and their internalised acceptance of those rules—in a sense completes the analytical circle. For Hart had set out to address three issues of perennial concern to jurisprudence. His nucleic expository theory attempts to explore those issues within a frame of reference in which the core elements of each issue are unravelled, defined, clarified and elucidated as a basis for attaining an improved and more complete understanding of the nature of municipal law.

To the question of how law and legal obligation differ from and are related to the "Austinian" model of habitually obeyed coercive commands of the sovereign, Hart points to, among other things: key differences between commands and more complex types of legal rules, differentiating duty-imposing from power-conferring rules; and the internal attitude of acceptance on the part of private citizens of primary rules which supplants the—as Hart portrays it—unthinking habit of obedience to commands of a sovereign. The legislature and other points of origin of legal rules supplant the sovereign as a source of laws. In a modern municipal legal system the existence of a rule of recognition—not the existence of a determinate individual acting in the role of sovereign—unifies the legal system under the aegis of officially recognised and internally accepted criteria for the identification of the primary rules of the system. Law is structured not as a plurality of situational commands but as the interplay between two types of rules: primary rules in general,

---

[55] *PTL*, 80.

regulating the behaviour of private citizens, and secondary rules, regulating official conduct.

To the question, "how does law differ from, and how is it related to, moral obligation?", Hart asks us to see the rule of recognition as the key factor differentiating legal rules from any other rules that could function as social rules in the life of a community: for example, moral precepts or rules of etiquette.

To the question "what are rules and to what extent is law an affair of rules?", Hart provides the answer that legal rules are both duty-imposing and power-conferring and fulfil entirely distinct social functions corresponding to that distinction. But in any event rules differ from coercive orders in the "Austinian" sense in a number of respects which Hart specifies in the course of his detailed analysis. Furthermore, and crucially, law is to be seen as a union of primary rules (of obligation) and secondary rules of recognition, change and adjudication. The internal aspect of these rules—a critical reflective attitude towards relevant rule-governed behaviour and by and large acceptance of the relevant governing rules—on the part of the citizenry and officials in different ways underpins the entire legal process.

A basis for critique

The broad and simplifying discussion of Hart's theory of law in this chapter—specifically, the analytical nucleus of *The Concept of Law*—is the basis for a critique to follow in chapter 4. In the critique I intend, among other things, to reflect upon some of the ways in which Hart's perceived sociological isolationism and other significant factors—for instance, Hart's failure in some instances to pursue sociological enquiry sufficiently far—may have "problematised" or weakened key facets of his theory of law. The more fundamental objective of the critique is to advance towards a tentative outline—attempted in chapters 5, 6 and 7—of ways in which a theory of law might aim to surmount the problematical areas, so-called "Gordian Knots", identified in chapter 4.

4

Three Gordian Knots

". . . I think that no candid student of sociology could deny that, valuable as the insights have been which it has provided, the average book written in the sociological vein . . . is full of unanalyzed concepts and ambiguities. . . . Both psychology and sociology are relatively young sciences with an unstable framework of concepts and a correspondingly uncertain and fluctuating terminology." *H L A Hart*[1]

Three Gordian Knots

In Greek mythology it is said that Alexander the Great cut the Gordian Knot with a sword in order to avoid the ignominy that might have resulted if he had failed to disentangle it. Unlike the King of Phrygia, who consciously designed the fabled knot as an intractable puzzle, the Gordian Knots of Hart's nucleic expository theory are in some respects an *unintended* result of Hart's theoretical endeavours. My aim in the discussion that follows is not to "cut" the Gordian Knots, as that would leave the underlying problematical areas unexamined. Rather, I must attempt, so far as possible, to unravel the metaphorical knots here in order to perceive more clearly the origins of the points of weakness and deficiencies that, I will

[1] H L A Hart, "Analytical Jurisprudence in Mid-Twentieth Century: A Reply to Professor Bodenheimer" (1957) 105 *University of Pennsylvania Law Review* 953 at 974. I cannot speculate on whether Hart's category of "average" books written in the sociological vein included Max Weber's encyclopaedic *Economy and Society*. What is certain, though, is that a version of Part I of Weber's *Economy and Society*, bearing the title *The Theory of Social and Economic Organization* (*TSEO*), was translated into English under the editorship of Talcott Parsons and produced in 1947, ten years before Hart made this observation.

maintain, have beset Hart's theory of law. It is also useful to examine ways in which Hart points towards, yet never fully reaches, a proper resolution of relevant problem areas. Listing them in the order to be discussed, I propose to examine the following three Gordian Knots:

- First: the problem of perspective;
- Second: the problem of "reductionism" to legal rules;
- Third: the problematic tendency to obscure relationality.

First Gordian Knot: The problem of perspective

Internal and External Points of View

A problematising aspect of Hart's sociological isolationism was alluded to in chapter 3 above. There, I observed that Hart often uses the viewpoint of a hypothetical "external observer"—the "extreme external point of view", as Hart calls it—as a theoretical perspective from which to characterise particular ways of viewing law, law-affected behaviour, or human behaviour generally. I noted that where the external observer is seen to adopt an extreme empiricist approach to the observation of human behaviour, he or she merely notes external regularities or repeated patterns of behaviour without in any sense engaging with the mental content or motivations of the subjects observed. Although this point of view is not especially significant in social theory terms—equating to a Comteian form of sociological positivism—what is more important is the recognition which Hart gives to a "weaker", or less "hard empiricist", version of the external observer's viewpoint: a non-extreme external point of view. This, as I suggested, is a point of view that may be capable of development towards that of the observer acting as social scientific investigator. Such an observer, adopting the role of "Hartian legal theorist", as Neil MacCormick puts it, is inclined to make appropriate linkages between on one hand, externally observable regularities of human behaviour and, on the other hand, mental content, motivations and so on: for example, using legal rules as a reference point for the orientation of that behaviour. As I previously indicated, the observer, in making a connection between rules and rule-compliant behaviour seeks to understand the rule-compliant behaviour, from the "internal" point of view of the actor. If developed towards Weberian sociology, such an observer may aspire to "value-freedom": in other words, he or she may seek to reproduce the perspective of the observed subject without in any sense sharing the convictions, commitment or value position of that subject.

Though redolent of a key aspect of Weber's social science methodology, Hart's approach is not pursued far enough into the realm of Weberian sociology whose major task, as we have seen, is to attempt the interpretive understanding of social action and the causal explanation of its course and effects. Weber's definition of "action" includes all human behaviour when and in so far as the acting individual attaches a subjective meaning to it. Human action is rendered understandable to social scientific enquiry if the subjective beliefs, volitions, intentions and motives of the acting individual are in some way unlocked or penetrated by the investigator. Whereas in his sociology Weber develops a method of reaching an understanding of subjective meaning at least partly through an empathic process, it is clear that for his part Hart merely *points towards* the possibility, *but fails to construct a coherent version*, of the viewpoint of the empathically sensitive, external observer. Such a perspective might be adopted by a sociologically inclined jurist.

In *The Concept of Law*[2] as originally published (i.e., the "pre-*Postscript*" version), Hart in fact failed to identify *himself*, acting in the role of jurist, with the external "observer" or external point of view, although he made frequent use of this device. The closest Hart came to this was his statement that "*we*" can, if we so choose, occupy the position of an "observer"—a "behaviourist" observer, as it happens—who is content merely to record regularities of observable behaviour. In other words "we" do not engage with internal processes or subjective meanings underlying that behaviour. But that, in any event, was Hart's "extreme" external point of view: hardly an appropriate point of view for a sociologically inclined jurist.[3] Hart comments in the following terms on the more promising viewpoint

---

[2] See H L A Hart, *The Concept of Law* (Clarendon Press, Oxford, 1961).

[3] *CL*, 89.

identified by Neil MacCormick as the "hermeneutic" or non-extreme external point of view:[4]

"For the observer may, without accepting . . . [social] rules himself, assert that the group accepts the rules, and thus may from outside refer to the way in which *they* are concerned with them from the internal point of view."

Only in the *Postscript* to *The Concept of Law*, written at the end of his career, did Hart meaningfully elaborate upon the "hermeneutic" external point of view in terms that for the first time identified *his* position as jurist—that of the "descriptive legal theorist"—with that point of view:[5]

"Of course a descriptive legal theorist does not as such himself share the participants' acceptance of the law in these ways, but he can and should describe such acceptance, *as indeed I have attempted to do in this book.* [i.e., in *The Concept of Law*] It is true that for this purpose the descriptive legal theorist must *understand* what it is to adopt the internal point of view and in that limited sense he must be able to put himself in the place of an insider; but this is not to accept the law or share or endorse the insider's internal point of view or in any other way to surrender his descriptive stance."

Until the publication of the *Postscript,* Hart had never actually presented the point of view which he refers to in the *Postscript* as that of the "descriptive legal theorist" as that which he—*Hart*—acting as jurist would choose to adopt. Nor, having chosen not to adopt or closely identify himself with that viewpoint, did he proffer it as the viewpoint of any sociologically inclined jurist *other than* Hart. Instead, in *The Concept of Law*, as originally published, he ascribed that viewpoint to hypothetical actors who—if Weber, say, were the analyst—might well have been *subjects* of Weber's investigation. That is the point at which methodological and substantive issues became confusingly merged. Thus, Hart remarks that in a

---

[4] *CL,* 89.

[5] Ibid., 242 (Hart's emphasis and emphasis added). See also Gerald J Postema's comments on "detached judgements" in his essay, "The Normativity of Law", in Ruth Gavison (ed.), *Issues in Contemporary Legal Philosophy: The Influence of H.L.A. Hart* (Clarendon Press, Oxford, 1987) (1992 paperback reprint), 81 *et seq.* See specifically 83–93.

society which lives by rules, there may be tension between those who accept and voluntarily co-operate in maintaining the rules, and those who "reject the rules and attend to them *only from the external point of view* as a sign of possible punishment".[6] Hart's external point of view, then, as originally conceived, was not a viewpoint consciously formulated for adoption by a sociologically inclined jurist. It was rather, for the most part, an ascribed viewpoint of the citizen or actor implicated in the flux of day-to-day community life who, for one reason or another, rejects the community's rules. Clearly, Hart sees no point of comparison between the position of an actor (such as a conscientious objector) who, from an "internal" viewpoint, rejects certain legal rules (e.g., enforced conscription), and the position of an actor who willingly accepts the same rules from a not dissimilar "internal" viewpoint. The major point of differentiation between the "internal" and "external" Hartian viewpoints appears to be the factual existence, or absence, of "acceptance" of relevant legal rules.

Hart's failure to pursue adequately the theoretical consequences of the external or any other nascent viewpoints to which he alludes is a critical weakness of *The Concept of Law*. While Hart may be credited for pointing legal theory in the direction of Weberian social theory, as MacCormick has argued he clearly missed an opportunity to formulate a viewpoint that might have served as a methodological standard for legal theory in the social theory context. What is specifically "problematic" about that is the perspectival muddle that, in the result, impairs what is a highly important element of Hart's concept of law: the key, albeit flawed, distinction between internal and external aspects of rules and their corresponding viewpoints.

Hart's Intellectual and Political Conservatism

A further aspect of the problem of perspective is *conservatism*. The charge that Hart's conception of law is tainted with intellectual and political conservatism has been made by more than one commentator in recent years. Essentially, the accusation of conservatism has its origins in the much wider critical context of law (and legal theory) as "ideology": a subject to which writers as diverse as Paul Hirst, Roger

[6] *CL*, 91 (emphasis added).

Cotterrell and Valerie Kerruish have contributed. The issue of conservatism—not the wider issue of "ideology", which is a major area of study in its own right—is visited briefly under this Gordian Knot. In the present context, the discussion will centre in particular upon criticisms articulated by Donald Galloway and, to a lesser extent, by Brendan Edgeworth.

Galloway believes that Hart offers an entrapped lawyer's perception of the social phenomenon of law. The nucleus of Hart's expository theory can be criticised for placing essentially "lawyeristic" distinctions, conceptual clarifications and refinements at the centre of the explanatory process: for example, perceiving law as (merely) a union of rules of the "primary" and "secondary" kind. Hart's theory, in Galloway's view, has a superficial appearance of objectivity, yet it is entirely the product of Hart's institutional perspective. Hart's implicit claim is that his concept of law is "the" (only) concept of law. Galloway believes that Hart's conception of the legal world derives from an inclination—which he ascribes to ordinary language philosophy—to reflect an uncritical "attitude of acceptance towards the dogma of the power holders" or "the dominant ideology".[7] What leads Galloway to this position? What features of *linguistic philosophy* make it intrinsically conservative, and is this accusation tenable in its own right and when followed through into Hart's philosophy of law?

According to Galloway, the influence of Ludwig Wittgenstein on Hart is marked but largely unacknowledged.[8] Galloway claims that it was Wittgenstein's aim to formulate a philosophical approach to the *description* rather than the *interpretation* of the world.[9] Unlike

[7] Donald C Galloway, "The Axiology of Analytical Jurisprudence: A Study of the Underlying Sociological Assumptions and Ideological Predilections", in Thomas W Bechtler (ed.), *Law in a Social Context: Liber Amicorum Honouring Professor Lon L. Fuller* (Kluwer, The Netherlands, 1978), 49 at 74.

[8] Ibid., 64. See also Neil MacCormick, *H.L.A. Hart* (Edward Arnold (Publishers) Ltd., London, 1981), 15. MacCormick notes that the work of Hart's colleague, J L Austin, paralleled and converged with the work of Ludwig Wittgenstein, published as *Philosophical Investigations* (Basil Blackwell, Oxford, 1958).

[9] See A C Grayling, *Wittgenstein* (Oxford University Press, Oxford, 1988) (1996 reissue), 67 *et seq.*, but esp. 69. For further discussion of how Wittgenstein's work might be said to have influenced, or paralleled, Hart's thinking, see Wayne Morrison, *Jurisprudence: From the Greeks to Post-modernism* (Cavendish Publishing Ltd., London, 1997), 361–6.

interpretation, description in Galloway's view has a nuance of objectivity. Wittgenstein's approach sought to cure conceptual puzzlements which arise when language is misused. Confusion occurs most often when expressions are abstracted from their usual contexts and studied in isolation, or when there is a failure to recognise the multifarious uses of language. As Galloway puts it, when the "therapy" had been successful, "the puzzlement will disappear, as will all philosophical debates and disputes". In this respect, the philosopher was akin to a "doctor". Galloway refers to Bertrand Russell's criticism of linguistic philosophy's eschewal of theory, its refusal to postulate theories about reality or to question the *a priori* premises of science. Moreover, philosophically significant questions of the past were either marginalised or completely disregarded. Galloway makes much of Wittgenstein's philosophical predilection towards leaving the world "as it is", merely describing what is there by examining or clarifying the uses of language, a concomitant of this being the rejection of all philosophical speculation.[10]

This aspect of Wittgenstein's conservatism in Galloway's view gains support from his standpoint on the nature of language as a form of life and shared means of communication, involving generally agreed rules which one cannot look behind for explanation or justification. Galloway believes that it is always essential to look behind the words used in particular contexts. He demonstrates with two examples that frequently, without misdescribing a factual state of affairs, "one can make words mean what one wants them to mean, or allow them to embody values which other users of the word may not share".[11] First, the participants in essentially the same "language game" (as Wittgenstein called it)—for example reporting a battle—may *choose* which language to use and the rules to be followed. So although the same situation is being described, the language used may also *interpret* it, suggesting the introduction of a personal viewpoint. Thus, an uninvolved reporter may simply refer to the overall death toll in the aftermath of the battle. A politician on one side of the conflict may refer to the continuation of the struggle for liberation from aggression. Finally, a scientist may speak of the technical effectiveness of the weaponry used. None of

[10] See Wittgenstein, *Philosophical Investigations*, above at n. 8, 47 and 49.

[11] Galloway, above at n. 7, at 70–1.

the observers actually misdescribes what is happening, but each starts with a different picture of the world which reflects personal interests, beliefs and preconceptions.[12] Secondly, the identification of the meaning of a word with its use means that a *minority* use of a word will often appear abnormal, i.e., it will involve a misunderstanding of meaning and so constitute an unacceptable language game. The danger here is that from Wittgenstein's standpoint a minority "could never claim correctly that a majority were misusing a word".[13] For example, a minority group's perception of the "injustice" of a political system may be thought (by the majority) to involve misuse of the concept of injustice.

Galloway accepts Ernest Gellner's view that the kind of concepts and models that we use to describe things carry with them their own values, preferences and suggested directions.[14] Galloway concludes that if persuasive elements and preferences can enter our concepts, then the analysis of ordinary language can only lead to a view of the world through the eyes of those whose language one is studying. At the same time, claims of neutrality are illusory, while definitions which appear to be purely descriptive are not "non-committal".[15] Even in cases where there appear to be unified experience and a significant measure of value-sharing the potent force of language may in fact have served to "permeate the consciousness that leads to agreement".[16] Galloway warns that this is especially true of the use of language as a manipulative tool in political discourse.[17] Thus, the "result of accepting ordinary language as correct is a form of conservatism". By refusing to propose theory or to question or look behind the official ideology, the linguistic philosopher, according to Galloway's colourful phraseology, "willingly places his hands in the manacles of domination, and is passively led into "the official reality", without the thought of illusion or mirage entering his head".[18]

[12] Ibid., 68.

[13] Ibid., 69.

[14] Ibid., 71, quoting Ernest Gellner, *Words and Things* (Harmondsworth: Penguin Books, 1959), esp. 100, 158–9 and 256 *et seq.*

[15] Galloway, above at n. 7, at 71.

[16] Ibid., 72.

[17] Ibid., 73.

[18] Ibid., 74.

In essence, Galloway believes that the conservatism which besets ordinary language philosophy permeates Hart's conception of law in a number of ways. Galloway highlights, among others, the deficiencies outlined in chapter 3 in support of his critical stance.[19] Edgeworth similarly identifies a predisposition to conservatism in ordinary language philosophy which, in his view, arises from a tendency to preserve descriptions of the world which have become established by constant use and have stood the test of time. Adopting a similar stance to that of Galloway, Edgeworth argues that a major limitation of the approach is that there is no such thing as an absolute identifiable ordinary language purified of scientific conceptions and misconceptions, cultural and political attainments, prejudices and predispositions that have become "current" in the flux and struggle of day-to-day life. Thus, Hart, according to Edgeworth, simply and uncritically "raises to the status of absolute truth the prevailing ideologies of the day".[20]

Edgeworth emphasises that the need for *theory* is not supplanted. Following a distinctly "Weberian" line of argument, he maintains that it is always necessary to extract from a vast multiplicity of facts some which are relevant and others which are not. A theory is needed to propose what is to count as a relevant fact. In Edgeworth's view, the ordinary language philosopher has no method or criteria to govern the selection of relevant, and rejection of irrelevant, facts. The defect of *The Concept of Law* is its presumption of one correct appropriate common use.

What, then, is the force of these criticisms? Let us examine five aspects of this critique.

First criticism

It must firstly be questioned, without necessarily *defending* the ordinary language approach, whether the validity of many of the criticisms actually lies more in perceived deficiencies in the specifics of Hart's analysis than in the ordinary language philosophical

---

[19] Some of these criticisms, or points, are identified by attribution in the text or in textual notes.

[20] See Brendan Edgeworth, "Legal Positivism and the Philosophy of Language: A Critique of H.L.A. Hart's 'Descriptive Sociology'" (1986) 6 *Legal Studies* 115 at 122.

approach as such. Galloway fails to establish a *necessary* connection between the study of "ordinary language" as an approach to the analysis of (for example) law or polity, and the study of official or institutional language. Galloway mistakenly believes that because *Hart's* ordinary language approach evidently directs attention towards the "ordinary" language and concepts used by lawyers, judges and other officials working within the system, this is an essential consequence of such an approach. Is an ordinary language approach to law, in other words, ineluctably committed to an examination of *institutional* language and only institutional language? Certainly, Galloway identifies a number of tendencies—for example, the absence of theoretical speculation, leaving the world "as it is", shunning minority language usage—which make it more likely than not that a legal philosopher might adopt an institutional point of view, possibly inadvertently, and thereby diminish the importance of competing perspectives. When Hart apparently adopts such a viewpoint—in a sense, that of "received wisdom" as to what the law is—Galloway is able to assert that this is the natural and inevitable result of the ordinary language approach. Accusations of non-objectivity and arbitrariness follow close behind, and the entire Hartian apparatus appears to collapse.

Hart is admittedly open to criticism in so far as he fails to recognise or make explicit the extent to which his concept of law *is* that of an institutional insider. Yet there is every reason to suppose that an institutional point of view—appropriately identified and given a proper theoretical context—can be as valid and important a point of view as any other. Moreover, it is false to suggest that an institutional perspective cannot claim to be as "objective" as any other perspective. Why can there not be an institutional perspective which, whatever the methodological difficulties, seeks "objectivity"? Why is it not legitimate to turn our attention to the "ordinary language" of the institution as a focus of theoretical interest? Equally, is there any feature of the ordinary language approach which prevents the possibility of studying the "ordinary language" not only of the institution, but of *anyone* considered of significance for purposes of our study? If the principal aims of ordinary language philosophy are, first, to concentrate on language as a pathway to the objective description of the world and, secondly, to clarify conceptual obscurities arising through misuse of language, the study of (say) the "ordinary language" of an oppressed minority group, is not ruled out: but neither is the study of the "ordinary language" of the institution. There is nothing intrinsic to the notion of leaving the world "as it is" that prevents a conception of the world *"as it is" to an oppressed minority group* for instance being expressed through that group's world view and given the scrutiny afforded by an ordinary language methodology.

Second criticism

As Edgeworth suggests, there is a continuing need to theorise and to look behind language used (for example "law", "rule", "right", "power", "coercion"), particularly when it may be inherently theory-laden and not necessarily fully understood by the user, not least the institutional insider. The claim that Hart is in general *atheoretical* is false, however. It is obvious that the most influential component of Hart's work is *theory*. Even if Edgeworth is correct in suggesting that ordinary language philosophy has failed to provide a method of discriminating between significant and insignificant "facts", that clearly did not prevent Hart from selecting "facts" which supported or constituted his main theoretical conclusions: for example, that there exist primary and secondary rules, and that secondary rules are divisible into rules of recognition, adjudication and change. The problem of selecting matters of factual significance from the "infinitude" of social reality is not a problem unique to Hart or to ordinary language philosophers. It was a matter of particular concern to Weber.[21] We might ask how defensible is Edgeworth's seemingly "arbitrary" decision to focus on legal positivism and the philosophy of language as an object of critical attention. No more or less defensible, it would seem, than Hart's decision to focus on the work of John Austin for his critique, or to seize upon "facts" which appeared to support his dichotomy of primary and secondary rules.

[21] See especially the brief discussion of the doctrine of value-relevance (*Wertbeziehung*) in ch. 2 above.

Third criticism

Galloway and Edgeworth have rightly exposed a weakness of Hart's general approach. It is surely necessary in the context of legal philosophy to identify whether a particular world view is in fact that of a dominant or ruling group, or is a refraction of the conceptual apparatuses and linguistic devices used by that group to make sense of the world, or to constitute that world view. Whether Galloway and Edgeworth have correctly identified the origins of this weakness is less certain. It may be that in certain respects they are partly right and partly wrong. As I have suggested, it seems implausible to lay the blame for Hart's narrow viewpoint at the door of ordinary language philosophy. But other factors may have played a role here. If, on the one hand, Hart's adoption of an institutional insider's point of view involved an arbitrary, or misleadingly unacknowledged, narrowing of parameters of *factual significance*, then Hart, as we have seen, was in some measure "guilty". In that regard Edgeworth has correctly identified this as a core problem. On the other hand, whilst it is clear—*contra* Galloway and Edgeworth—that Hart "theorises", it may be that in many instances he fails to pursue theoretical tasks to an appropriate end. For instance, although Hart at times recognises the validity of competing viewpoints in *The Concept of Law* beyond those of "insiders" and "outsiders"[22] he conspicuously fails to identify and *render explicit* the viewpoint—that of an "institutional insider"—from which his nucleic expository theory largely emanates. He also fails to defend that viewpoint and does not attempt to set up theoretical perspectives in opposition or counterpoint to his institutional perspective: for example, that of a disadvantaged indigenous community.

Fourth criticism

There is no good reason to maintain that an institutional viewpoint is indefensible. It may be an error to present the legal world from a "lawyeristic", institutional perspective as if that exhaustively constitutes the world "as it is"—the only legitimate world view. Furthermore, if an institutional perspective is adopted, *that in itself*

[22] For example, that of the "bad man", "puzzled man", "ignorant man": see *CL*, 40.

should be justified. One reason for adopting such a viewpoint (for example, that of a judge) is that within a community, certain coercive forces which exercise significant social power are mobilised solely on the direction of a court or tribunal. If coercive apparatuses are kept in check by an interposing mechanism regulating the exercise of that power, it makes sense to seek a preliminary understanding of this form of social power from the point of view of those who control and exercise it.

A clear delineation of an institutional perspective may also furnish a basis for a focused comparative study of competing perspectives. For example, the viewpoint of an indigenous or tribal community denied land rights despite the existence of "legal protections" accentuates the gap between legal image and reality.[23] There may thus be a compelling *moral* justification for constructing an institutional viewpoint when, against the background of an oppressed or disenfranchised minority group's aspirations, it throws into sharp relief a ruling group's hegemonic presumptions. An understanding of institutions which wield significant power, and of the power itself, is a necessary condition of reaching a proper understanding of institutional structures of domination and oppression. We can only assess the deficiencies of the institutional world view when it can be tested against the world view of other groups. That, of course, is not Hart's primary concern in *The Concept of Law*, but his institutional perspective or some elaboration of that perspective may be a useful starting point.

Fifth criticism

Finally, can it be said that, as a methodological technique, the study of ordinary language as such is flawed or misconceived? The views of Galloway and Edgeworth are very clear in highlighting limitations of this technique and provide grounds for exercising caution in using, and in evaluating the results of the use of, this approach. But, more importantly, is this technique—or more specifically Hart's hermeneutic approach—incompatible with Weberian social theory? It is clear that in certain respects Hart's "hermeneutic"

[23] The position of Latin America's forest-dwellers, the Brazilian and Venezuelan Yanomami, can be mentioned here. See Roger Plant, *Land Rights and Minorities* (Minority Rights Group International Report, 1994), 13.

approach is entirely compatible with Weber. The "Weberian" social scientist seeks to objectify the meaning of the behaviour of the observed subject. How else can this be accomplished—or at least approached—except through an examination of what the German philosopher, Wilhelm Dilthey, called the "expressions" of the actor? What better "Diltheian expressions" can there be but the "ordinary"—which, in a legal context, may often mean "technical"—language used by the subject of the investigation? [24]

Second Gordian Knot: The problem of "reductionism" to legal rules

The Second Gordian Knot potentially raises issues of importance not merely in the arena of sociology of law but also in analytical jurisprudence, for it has been questioned whether it is at all tenable to maintain that a municipal legal system is in reality constituted by a combination of primary and secondary rules as Hart presents these.[25] If law *is* an affair of rules or norms, what type(s) of rules or norms are they in functional and structural terms? In emphasising the importance of legal "principles", Dworkin has cast doubt upon Hart's notion of law as a system of (solely) rules.[26] Doubts have also been expressed as to the tenability of the functional distinctions which differentiate the three types of secondary rules. For example, MacCormick and others refer to the problem of seeming circularity in the interrelationship of secondary rules of recognition, change and adjudication.[27] Many specific criticisms have been directed towards the doctrine of the rule of recognition and other facets of Hart's theory from, as it were, *within* the discipline of ana-

[24] See, generally, ch. 2 above.

[25] C F H Tapper, "Powers and Secondary Rules of Change", in A W B Simpson (ed.), *Oxford Essays in Jurisprudence* (second series) (Clarendon Press, Oxford, 1973), 242 *et seq*. Rolf Sartorius also questions this: see R Sartorius, "The Concept of Law" (1966) 52 *Archiv für Rechts-und-Sozialphilosophie* 161 at 167.

[26] Ronald Dworkin, *Taking Rights Seriously* (Fifth Impression) (Gerald Duckworth & Co. Ltd., 1977), esp. 22–8.

[27] See Neil MacCormick, *H.L.A. Hart* (Edward Arnold (Publishers) Ltd., London, 1981), 108, and generally ch. 9.

lytical jurisprudence.[28] In the context of this, the Second, Gordian Knot, our attention is directed not towards issues that have already been the subject of extensive critical attention "within" the literature of analytical jurisprudence or its broader philosophical offshoots. Rather, it is intended to focus only upon issues which are taken to be the consequence of the sociologically isolationist frame of reference within which Hart theorises. In that context I propose to discuss here in broad outline Hart's misplaced emphasis on rules and its tendency to exclude consideration of law as a human behavioural phenomenon.

For Hart, law is quite certainly an affair of rules.[29] This is evident not only from his treatment of the specific question "to what extent is law an affair of rules?", but from the approach which he adopts to his two other recurrent questions, as we have seen in chapter 3 above. Such is the centrality of rules—and perceived attitudes towards rules—in *The Concept of Law*, that other issues which might be considered of equal importance are largely eclipsed. For Hart, the municipal law of a modern state comprises a system combining primary and secondary *rules*. The union of primary and secondary rules is "the heart of a legal system" and is "a most powerful tool for the analysis of much that has puzzled both the jurist and the political theorist".[30] The introduction of secondary *rules*—not the introduction of legal and political institutions (i.e., structures of official roles *organised by* rules)—is the remedy for tackling the claimed deficiencies of the hypothetical, pre-legal social environment: uncertainty, stasis and inefficiency.

With Hart, it is possible to perceive municipal law, at least in part, as a rule-governed activity not only at the "primary" level—the level of private citizens—but at the "secondary" level—the level of judges, police and other state officials. But against Hart, as I have previously noted, it is necessary to perceive law as a human—and to an extent, though not exhaustively, an *institutional*—activity. Of course, Hart does not consider law to be anything other than an

---

[28] See, for example Rolf Sartorius, "Hart's Concept of Law", in Robert S Summers (ed.), *More Essays in Legal Philosophy* (Basil Blackwell, Oxford, 1971), 131 *et seq.*

[29] See *CL*, 13.

[30] Ibid., 98.

activity involving human beings. Nor is he unaware of its institutional nature. The one presupposition that consistently underlies Hart's concept of law is that of the institutional context of law. But Hart's approach primarily emphasises that an improved understanding of law is to be reached through meticulous conceptual analysis: the rigorous examination of rules and other normative constructs.

If Hart's claim that *The Concept of Law* is "an essay in descriptive sociology" were to have been taken seriously, should not its theoretical emphasis have inclined more markedly towards one of the primary concerns of sociology: social *action*? As we have seen, Weberian sociology aims to reach an interpretive understanding of social action and its underlying subjective states in order to explain action in causal terms. If understanding and explaining human behaviour is the central task of Weberian sociology, attaining an understanding of the social action comprised in institutional and other relevant law-affected behaviour is merely incidental to Hart's enterprise. It is by no means his main concern.

It is, moreover, a curious distortion to look upon rules—rather than human behaviour—as having an "internal aspect". Hart oscillates confusingly between the notion of the "internal aspect of rules" and the "internal point of view", and between both those notions, on the one hand, and the "critical reflective attitude" to rules, on the other. The internal aspect is, however, repeatedly presented as an aspect "of rules", although essentially Hart analyses this in terms of complexes of *attitudes towards* rules. Thus, relevant attitudes towards rules can be seen as part of the internal aspect of human behaviour, which can be equated to the "subjective meaning" of behaviour, if we adopt Weber's terminology. To that extent, then, Hart strays slightly from an analysis focused upon rules, towards an analysis of social action manifested in attitudes to rules. But this is "sociological drift", not serious sociology, as Cotterrell points out.[31] It is difficult to break free from the notion, perpetuated in *The Concept of Law*, that everything that is puzzling—everything that stands in need of elucidation—in jurisprudence can be rendered explicable through the attainment of an understanding of

[31] See Roger Cotterrell, *The Politics of Jurisprudence: A Critical Introduction to Legal Philosophy* (Butterworths, London and Edinburgh, 1989), 96.

rules. It is difficult, in other words, once inside the theoretical edifice which Hart has constructed, to broaden the perspective to include law-affected human behaviour, or, more specifically, law-affected social action. Such a perspective could encompass consideration of the structure and functions of legal rules and legal systems, as Hart envisages; but it would additionally place at the centre of the analytical enterprise law-affected *behaviour* in general, and institutional *behaviour* in particular. The perspective of other groups—for example, that of ethnic minorities—and their law-affected behaviour would be equally important to such a venture. To be fair, Hart does indicate several "escape routes" out of his seemingly airtight world of conceptual analysis. As we have seen, his inchoate, "non-extreme" external (or "hermeneutic") point of view and rudimentary hermeneutic approach are two examples. To that extent Hart at least hesitantly points to a valid object of enquiry that is something other than rules and normative constructs. He alludes to a perspective which holds out the possibility of observing, and establishing a means of understanding, human behaviour.

Taking several steps back now, what can be said to account for this one-sided, somewhat distorting theoretical emphasis on legal rules? In *The Politics of Jurisprudence* Roger Cotterrell offers a compelling answer. Cotterrell argues that Hart's legal theory portrays law as a self-regulating system of rules. The rule of recognition and other rules are to be seen as governing the processes of production, interpretation, enforcement, amendment and repeal of rules within the legal system.[32] Cotterrell suggests that there is little room in this image of law for the Austinian notion of the legal order as an expression of political power: that of the sovereign. Hart's image of law is one in which *rules, rather than people, govern*. Rules govern the power-holders:[33]

"What is, indeed, implied here is an aspect of the deeply resonant political symbol so obviously missing from Austin's jurisprudence—

[32] Ibid., 99.

[33] Ibid. Galloway, above at n. 7, 81, makes an essentially similar point: "I must demonstrate that [Hart's] . . . theory does in fact, fail to explain, while attempting to promote, the values to which legal systems pretend to pledge their allegiance, namely, those inherent in polemics on existence of a government of laws rather than of men, and in the defence of 'apolitical' decision-making".

the symbol of the Rule of Law, a 'government of laws and not of men'."

According to Cotterrell, Hart's schema of "public" secondary rules typifies the modern constitutional state or *Rechtsstaat* in which the powers of officials are not arbitrary, but defined by rules of law. In the "private" sphere, power-conferring "facilitative" rules (e.g., contract laws) allow individuals freely and purposively to modify their legal position. These rules define the autonomy of the individual as a citizen and participant in the political community. The emerging image, thus, is of a constrained government subject to law counterpoised against an empowered, autonomous citizenry. Cotterrell believes that this image of law is politically more attractive in a modern democracy than the Austinian notion of subjection to a sovereign.[34]

Cotterrell points to the similarities between the Hartian and Kelsenian images of law which hold notwithstanding the radically different methods adopted by the two theorists. For Kelsen, as for Hart, there is a "special property unique to the law": "[T]he law governs its own creation. In particular, it is a legal norm that governs the process whereby another legal norm is created, and also governs—to a different degree—the content of the norm to be created".[35] So law governs its own creation, modification and destruction. The judicial decision—involving the creation of a concretised norm governing the particular circumstances to which the decision relates—is authorised by norms defining the court's jurisdiction. While Hart recognises judicial discretion as the "non-legal" element supplementing the legal element of rules, Kelsen is aware that law-applying judicial acts are partly determined by law and partly undetermined.[36] The non-legal determinants of new law—for Kelsen, politics—are beyond the scope of the pure theory. As Cotterrell observes, the pure theory is concerned only to know law, not politics or any considerations that may shape legal change or legal inter-

[34] Cotterrell, above at n. 31, at 100.

[35] Hans Kelsen, *Introduction to the Problems of Legal Theory* (Clarendon Press, Oxford, 1992) (*PTL*), 63.

[36] Cotterrell, above at n. 31, at 109.

pretation. Like Hart, Kelsen presents a view of law in which human beings have "almost disappeared":[37]

> "Thus law, as portrayed by Kelsen's normative legal theory, becomes a web of normative ideas from which human agency is excluded. Neither Kelsen nor Hart deny the human, creative element in law. But in neither theory is there a place to analyse it."

Cotterrell refers to this development in twentieth century positivist legal theory, using the words of the German jurist, Carl Schmitt: "The sovereign . . . the engineer of the great machine [of law], has been radically pushed aside. *The machine now runs by itself*".[38] Although neither Hart nor Kelsen explicitly advocates a rule of law conception of law, as Cotterrell points out, the common narrative of an impersonal, de-politicised normative order excludes any acknowledgement that law is an expression of political power. The implicit claim that this is an appropriate way to view law goes hand in hand with the latent suggestion that law as an autonomous intellectual field can have a unity, systematicity and integrity independent of politics. The rule of law idea is thus, "in some sense built into the very notion of law". On a sympathetic reading we might conclude, like Cotterrell, that it is a matter of great moral and political concern to Hart and Kelsen for law to be, and to be viewed as, a means of controlling and limiting arbitrary governmental power. It is thus necessary in Cotterrell's view to place the *Pure Theory of Law*[39] in the wider context of Kelsen's political writings in which, among other things, he defends the ideal of a democracy which is tolerant of the minority viewpoint. The "truth" of the knowledge-claims of the *Pure Theory of Law*, according to Cotterrell, are relative only to, and can only be evaluated within the context of, the limited field of enquiry and methods established for that unique science: legal science. Similarly, *The Concept of Law* is

[37] Ibid., 112. In a parallel analysis, Galloway suggests that "[t]he constitution assumes such importance in Hart's eyes that the officials whom it controls, blend into the hazy background, while rules adopt the role of protagonist" (above at n. 7, at 84).

[38] Cotterrell, above at n. 31, at 112 (emphasis added).

[39] Above at n. 35.

ideally to be seen in the broader context of Hart's commitment to liberal individualism and hostility to authoritarianism.[40]

Yet we might alternatively conclude, less sympathetically, that if a theory simply fails to fit the facts or implicitly, yet mistakenly, claims to represent the "natural order of things", or falsely claims to account for all manifestations of the phenomena under consideration, or one-sidedly emphasises one feature whilst de-emphasising other significant features, accusations of distortion and error are sure to be made, and with some justification.[41] It is clear that the position of human behaviour—that is, social, but particularly institutional action and other law-affected behaviour—must be established more emphatically at the centre of the positivist enterprise. Otherwise, there is a price to be paid. *Distortion* is the price of a rule-centred, de-personalised image of law.

Third Gordian Knot: The problematic tendency to obscure relationality

An important corollary of Hart's inclination to render human beings "invisible" is the virtual "disappearance" of *relationality* as a characteristic of the legal universe. The Second and Third Gordian Knots thus have a common origin in the problem of "reductionism". I previously noted that Hart's focus upon rules had obscured the relational dimension of human behaviour and had de-emphasised one of its most critical dynamics: social power. It is surprising that Hart should have described *The Concept of Law* as an essay in (descriptive) sociology when he expended so little effort on exploring a dimension of law—social power—that would be a natural preoccupation of any "orthodox" sociologist. For instance, Weber reminds us that social power is first and foremost a relational medium.[42] If we conceive of legal phenomena as ultimately

[40] Cotterrell, above at n. 31, at 116.

[41] What criteria can be applied in assessing a theory? See Tom Campbell, *Seven Theories of Human Society* (Clarendon Press, Oxford, 1981), 25 *et seq*; see esp. 43–50 where, among the criteria for critically evaluating theories of society, Campbell lists empirical adequacy and explanatory adequacy: "Theories must not only fit the facts of social life, they must also explain them" (47).

[42] *ES*, 1378 (*Herrschaft*). See also ES 212–3. For further discussion in this book, see chapter 7.

reducible to legal rules—or give this reductionism undue prominence—there is a risk of concealing or distorting what is truly social
about human social behaviour—its relational, interactional quality.
The American sociologist Talcott Parsons has particularly emphasised the relational aspect of social action:[43]

"Since a social system is a system of processes of interaction between
actors, it is the structure of the *relations* between the actors as
involved in the interactive process which is essentially the structure
of the social system. The system is a network of such relationships."

At several points in his *General Theory of Law*, the Russian jurist
N M Korkunov demonstrated that he had grasped the essential cor-
respondence between legal and social relationships. Whilst he did
not attempt a sociological analysis of law based on the notion of
social relationality, he advanced the view that legal relations are
social relations "but governed by a legal rule".[44] He argued that
social relationships are transformed into legal relationships by
means of the conceptual apparatus of rights and duties:[45]

"[Human beings] . . . so far as they aid themselves by legal rules,
transform their social relations into legal ones, social dependence into
a legal obligation, and the power of influence which they have over
each other into rights."

Korkunov's stance led him to the view that not only is every legal
relationship composed of a right and a duty[46] but also that legal
relationships subsist only between natural and juridical persons: not
between persons and *things*. That position was a concomitant of his
more general stance according to which legal relationships were to
be seen as "juridicised" social relationships. Korkunov held that
legal relations exist "not between an individual and a thing but only
between several individuals on account of the use of a thing".[47]

---

[43] Talcott Parsons, *The Social System* (The Free Press, New York, 1951), 25.
See also Talcott Parsons, Edward A Shils *et al* (eds.), *Toward a General Theory
of Action* (Harvard University Press, Cambridge, Mass., 1951), 61–2.

[44] N M Korkunov, *General Theory of Law* (The Boston Book Company [The
Modern Legal Philosophy Series, Vol. IV], 1909), 192.

[45] Ibid., 195.

[46] Ibid., 199.

[47] Ibid., 201.

This cleared the way for his more fundamental position on the nature of legal relationships as essentially social relationships: "Legal relations, it is readily seen, are possible, then, only between individuals. Only individuals can be subjects of juridical relations. They alone are capable of them".[48]

Korkunov may have been right to insist that the only "true" legal relationships are essentially social relationships defined by legal norms. But that is not to say that a relationship—even a relationship endowed with legal significance—cannot exist between individuals and inanimate objects. Human beings *do* factually perceive themselves as standing in a relation to inanimate objects and this is reflected in language such as "this is mine", "that is hers", and so on. This use of language undeniably asserts a relationship between a person and a thing which is so compelling that the law cannot lightly disregard it. Person–thing relationships are thus all-pervasive within the law, but it is beyond the scope of this book to dwell further on that important category of relationships.

Korkunov nonetheless—and, in a slightly different context, as we will find in chapter 7, W N Hohfeld and Albert Kokourek—happen to give prominence to person–person relationships. In *The Concept of Law* Hart—largely neglecting Weberian sociology and the work of Hohfeld and of jurists such as Korkunov—merely gives superficial attention to the relational component of law. Hart mentions only in passing that the figure of a bond binding the person obligated (buried in the word "obligation": Latin, *ligare*, to bind) "haunts much legal thought". In Hart's extended metaphor, social pressure is manifested as a chain binding those who have obligations so that they are not free to do what they want. In the criminal law context the other end of the chain may be held by officials who insist on performance or exaction of a penalty. In the sphere of civil law a private individual "having rights correlative to the obligations" may hold the chain and has a choice whether or not to insist on performance or its equivalent in value.[49] Hart's dual classification of legal rules as "duty-imposing" and "power-conferring" furthermore perpetuates an asymmetrical view of legal rules that stresses the superordinate side of power-conferring rules and the subordinate or

[48] Ibid., 201.
[49] *CL*, 87–8. See also Hart's comments in textual note to p. 27 at *CL*, 284.

subjectional side of duty-imposing rules. The possibility of relationality and its underlying notion of correlativity—that there is *another side* to what is in fact a relationship—is unwittingly concealed by this use of terminology. Hart's use of language is, in other words, entirely consistent with an explanatory approach that fails to emphasise not merely the *analytical* importance of relationality—an error in itself, given the manifest importance of Hohfeld's analysis—but also its *sociological* significance.

The three Gordian Knots in retrospect

If we were to display more generosity towards Hart than Hart displayed (say) towards John Austin, we might conclude from the three Gordian Knots that they are the record of only a *partial* failure. For the underlying problems contain many of the seeds of their own resolution. That that is emphatically true of key aspects of Hart's nucleic expository theory should be clear from the preceding discussion. Of course it would be fanciful to suggest that because it possesses "failings", Hart's theory lacks explanatory power. The theory is merely vitiated to the extent of its "failings". It is possible to argue that certain constructively modified elements of Hart's theory—key insights of Hartian jurisprudence—may be incorporated within a sociologically more informed variant of his theory. As that is beyond the scope of this book, however, we might instead ask more generally whether there is a plausible means of approaching theoretical enquiry into law which surmounts the problems of the three Gordian Knots. In chapters 5, 6 and 7 I will lay the groundwork for that enquiry by attempting to suggest where the beginnings of a resolution of each of the Gordian Knots might lie.

5
Perspectives Redefined

"What *actually* happens in a group owing to the *probability* that persons engaged in social action (*Gemeinschaftshandeln*), especially those exerting a socially relevant amount of power, subjectively consider certain norms as valid and practically act according to them, in other words, orient their own conduct towards these norms?" *Max Weber*[1]

The first Gordian Knot revisited

The problem of perspective or point of view, discussed under the first Gordian Knot—which, among other things, exposed Hart to the accusation of conservatism—manifested itself in two ways which can be distinguished at methodological and substantive levels.

1. At a *methodological* level, Hart merely pointed towards the possibility, but failed to construct, a coherent version of the viewpoint of an empathically sensitive external observer: a viewpoint that might possibly have equated to that of a "sociologically inclined jurist". The confusion in Hart's analysis was underlined by his conflation of methodological and substantive aspects of the viewpoints to which he alluded.

An examination of the role assigned to the social scientific investigator in Weber's methodological writings might be the basis of a practical enquiry into how the *jurist* might perform such a role in the context of an analysis of law as a social phenomenon. In the next section of this chapter I will attempt merely to initiate such an enquiry using Weber's sociological point of

[1] Max Weber, *Economy and Society. An Outline of Interpretive Sociology* (Bedminster Press Inc., New York, 1968) (*ES*), 311; Max Weber, *Max Weber on Law in Economy and Society* (Harvard University Press, Cambridge, Mass., 1954) (*LES*), 11 (Weber's emphasis).

view as a point of departure referring back, at appropriate points, to the discussion of Weber in chapter 2 above.

2. At a *substantive* level, Hart failed to delineate satisfactorily, or even to acknowledge explicitly, the "insider's" viewpoint from which his concept of law largely emanated. Presented essentially in terms of the "lawyeristic" device of the union of primary and secondary rules, Hart's concept of law was thus conceived both:

   (a) from the "internal" point of view of a citizenry who, by and large, "accept" the law as expressed in primary rules; and
   (b) from the "internal" point of view of judges and other officials who "accept" the law as expressed in secondary rules.

   Hart also failed to defend his adopted viewpoints or to set up theoretical perspectives in counterpoint to those viewpoints. A theory of law might surmount this problem by defining more explicitly, but also defending, the point of view of an "institutional insider".

   In the third section of this chapter I will attempt to outline such a point of view by formulating an ideal type theoretical construct in the Weberian sense that reproduces aspects of the viewpoint of a hypothetical ultimate judge, *Iudex*. Such an institutional perspective might be applied as a basis for considering and contrasting "non-institutional" perspectives, though it is beyond the scope of this book to examine such contrasting perspectives.

The sociologically inclined jurist

The first task is to consider in outline a few aspects of a unique role: that of the jurist acting as social scientific investigator. For reasons to be clarified it is useful, as I have mentioned, to take Weber's sociological point of view as a point of departure. Knowledge of the legal world may be seen to be refracted through this prismatic point of view. Law is rendered understandable both as a social and as a juridical phenomenon.

The Sociological Point of View

For Weber, all knowledge of cultural reality was knowledge from particular points of view. Weber considered it to be an elementary requirement that the historian and social research worker should distinguish the important from the trivial, and that for this purpose they should adopt a particular point of view. The point of view would enable, as Weber put it, a selection to be made of a tiny portion of the "absolute infinity" with which the investigator is concerned.[2] In the opening paragraphs of the *Sociology of Law*,[3] Weber draws his key distinction between the sociological and the juridical points of view.

The juridical point of view is that of "legal dogmatics" (*dogmatische Rechtswissenschaft*) or jurisprudence.[4] The idea of "legal dogmatics" was also the subject of an important distinction made by Hans Kelsen. Kelsen had distinguished between "legal dogmatics" (using the expression "*Rechtsdogmatik*") and general legal theory. For Kelsen, however, the focal concern of legal dogmatics was narrow—the interpretation of specific provisions of particular legal systems.[5] Weber's conception of "legal dogmatics", using the expression "*Rechtswissenschaft*" ("legal science"), suggests Kelsen's narrower sense but could extend into areas which, ironically, come within the realm of *general legal theory* in Kelsen's sense (*allgemeine Rechtslehre*). Weber's juridical point of view does have some of the characteristics of Kelsen's narrow category of "legal dogmatics". For instance, this point of view, according to Weber, asks what significance or normative meaning ought to be attributed in correct logic to a verbal pattern having the form of a legal proposition. It

[2] See Max Weber, " 'Objectivity' in Social Science and Social Policy", in Max Weber, *The Methodology of the Social Sciences* (The Free Press, New York, 1949) (*OSS*), 81–2. See also John Finnis, *Natural Law and Natural Rights* (Clarendon Press, Oxford, 1980), 11–15.

[3] Weber, *LES*, above at n. 1.

[4] *ES*, 311; *LES*, 11. According to Max Rheinstein, the expression "legal dogmatics" has frequently been used in German to mean "the legal science of the law itself as distinguished from such ways of looking upon law from the outside as philosophy, history, or sociology of law" (*ES*, 337, n. 1; *LES*, 11, n. 2).

[5] See Hans Kelsen, *Introduction to the Problems of Legal Theory* (Clarendon Press, Oxford, 1992) (*PTL*), 128.

also aims to discover "the correct meaning of propositions the content of which constitutes an order supposedly determinative for the conduct of a defined group of persons: in other words, it tries to define the facts to which this order applies and the way in which it bears upon them".[6] But the wider sense of Weber's juridical point of view carries the notion more recognisably into the domain of general legal theory:[7]

"[T]he jurist, taking for granted the empirical validity of the legal propositions, examines each of them and tries to determine its logically correct meaning in such a way that all of them can be combined in a system which is logically coherent, i.e., free from internal contradictions".

The systemic nature of law, therefore, which Kelsen would doubtless have regarded as the preserve of legal theory (in his sense) and not "legal dogmatics" (in his sense) could be, for Weber, the preserve of "legal dogmatics" in his wider usage of that expression. Weber sets up the sociological point of view in contrast to the juridical point of view and in so doing differentiates the aims of the sociology of law from his own notion of "legal dogmatics" in the sense which, as we have seen, possibly ventures into areas that fall within Kelsen's notion of general legal theory (*allgemeine Rechtslehre*).

The sociological point of view asks:[8]

"What *actually* happens in a group owing to the *probability* that persons engaged in social action (*Gemeinschaftshandeln*), especially those exerting a socially relevant amount of power, subjectively consider certain norms as valid and practically act according to them, in other words, orient their own conduct towards these norms?"

Crucially, Weber adds that a discipline such as sociology searches for empirical regularities and accordingly looks to the legal guarantees *and their underlying normative conceptions* as causes or consequences of these regularities.[9] Weber does not appear to recognise any inconsistency between the fact that he *contrasts* his

[6] *ES*, 311; *LES*, 11.
[7] *ES*, 311; *LES*, 11.
[8] *ES*, 311; *LES*, 11 (Weber's emphasis).
[9] *ES*, 331–2; *LES*, 33–4.

sociological point of view with his juridical point of view (corresponding to his sense of "legal dogmatics") and the fact that his sociology of law studies "underlying normative conceptions"—something to which "legal dogmatics" in Weber's (wide) sense arguably *could* extend. The point of contrast doubtless lies in the particularity of that *part* of "legal dogmatics" (in Weber's sense) which concerns itself with the interpretation of specific provisions of selected legal systems.

The recognition that the sociological point of view could concern itself with underlying normative conceptions—the natural preserve of general legal theory by *any* account—is revelatory. For it opens up the possibility of the types of conceptual analysis associated with analytical jurisprudence (including the type of conceptual analysis favoured by Hart) being relevant to, or capable of integration or repositioning within (at least) *Weberian* sociological enquiry. How does that possibility emerge?

In the first place, Weber's sociological point of view reinforces the possibility that at a certain level of analysis there may be no incompatibility between (legal) conceptual analysis and sociology: indeed, they may be *entirely compatible*. Thus, Martin Krygier notes that the conceptual distinctions, refinements and methods with which *The Concept of Law*[10] is concerned have *sociological* bearing and importance.[11] This is the sense in which Krygier believes that the book is "an essay in descriptive sociology". Krygier endorses Hart's suggestion that sociologists would do well to pay attention to the conceptual issues with which analytical jurists are concerned.[12] He points to the absurdity of a sociology of law which diminishes the importance of rigorous, conceptual analysis. There is no reason to believe that in principle the objectives of legal sociology are incompatible with a mode of conceptual analysis which seeks a sharpened awareness of words to enlighten our perception of phenomena. Taking up MacCormick's point,[13] Krygier argues that

[10] H L A Hart, *The Concept of Law* (Clarendon Press, Oxford, 2nd ed. 1994) (*CL*).

[11] Martin Krygier "*The Concept of Law* and Social Theory" (1982) 2 *Oxford Journal of Legal Studies*, 155 at 159.

[12] Ibid., 160.

[13] Ibid. See Neil MacCormick, "Challenging Sociological Definitions" (1977) 4 *British Journal of Law and Society*, 87.

sociology of law must begin with conceptual analysis and return to it continually. More broadly, Krygier argues that not only is conceptual analysis important for a social theory of law, but an adequate conceptual base is no less important for empirical work.[14]

In the second place, as I noted in chapter 4 above, coercive forces wielding significant social power in a community—powers defined in and regulated by laws—are normally kept in check and are controlled by an interposing apparatus of courts and tribunals. A preliminary understanding of such power may be sought from the point of view of those who control and exercise it, for example judges and others involved in applying and enforcing the law. Weber's sociological point of view does give precedence to the study of "those exerting a socially relevant amount of power". The point of view of *Iudex*—to be discussed later in this chapter—happens to give priority to the point of view of a power holder, a judge, in order to elucidate aspects of the exercise of power from that point of view. But that is not to suggest that any other viewpoint is less worthy of attention, or is unimportant. It may simply be the object of a different, or separate, enquiry.

In the third place, Weberian sociology, as we have seen, is a science that attempts the interpretive understanding of social action in order to arrive at a causal explanation of its course and effects. Weber's sociological point of view exactly coincides with that scientific standpoint, for it asks what actually happens in a group owing to the probability that persons engaged in social action subjectively consider certain norms as valid and orient their conduct according to them. The causal task looks to empirical regularities and seeks to express these in terms of "probability". The interpretive task seeks an understanding of social action whose subjective meaning includes as a component *orientation by reference to valid legal norms*. In other words, a component of complexes of motivations and other mental processes that determine behaviour is orientation of social action by reference to legal norms. Thus, the science of sociology aims among other things to reach an understanding of the subjective meaning of human social action. It makes the official behaviour of those who wield significant power in society, such as judges and officials, a particular—though not the sole—object of

[14] Martin Krygier, above at n. 11, at 160.

interest. Judges and officials largely, yet not exhaustively, orient their official behaviour—"social action" in Weber's sense—by reference to legal norms. In other words, they use or follow legal norms in the course of discharging their official functions. Those norms feature as part of the complex of mental processes by which they modify or orient their official behaviour: i.e., the norms are part of the "subjective meaning" of the social action of the judges and officials, to use Weber's terminology again.

Where, then, does *conceptual analysis* fit into this? Lawyers, judges and officials do not often use simple, individuated legal norms as guides for the orientation of their official behaviour. More often than not the legal material that is relevant in a particular instance comes in the form of complexes of interrelated norms rather than as simple imperatives such as "thou shalt . . ." or "thou shalt not . . .". Lawyers, judges and officials also use doctrines, principles, precedents and other normative conceptions and apply complex processes of judicial reasoning in the context of their decision-making processes. In order to reach a proper understanding of exercises of social legal power in judicial or official contexts as an integral part of sociological enquiry—in other words, to understand the "subjective meaning" of the relevant judicial or official behaviour—an understanding of the underlying *normative conceptions* is arguably essential, as Weber suggests and writers such as MacCormick and Krygier endorse.

In an influential essay published in 1966, Robert Summers identified the wider variety of analytical tasks being performed by "new jurists" such as Hart and Dworkin when compared with most jurists of the past, including John Austin.[15] Summers highlighted the main types of activity associated with the new jurists. He included: (i) analysis of the existing conceptual framework of and about law; and (ii) construction of new conceptual frameworks with accompanying terminologies. Summers noted that even in the context of the first activity—analysis of the conceptual *status quo*—which had been a preoccupation of earlier jurists, the new jurists were analysing a wider range of concepts at the same time as applying more sophisticated methodologies. In response to the question "what is

[15] R S Summers, "The New Analytical Jurists" (1966) 41 *New York University Law Review* 861.

conceptual analysis?", Summers echoed J L Austin's aphorism, subsequently taken up by Hart, that a sharpened awareness of the uses of words can sharpen our perception of phenomena. The importance of language lies in its role as the means of expression of legal concepts and ideas. But concepts and ideas currently used by laymen or professionals in dealing with law are the relevant *subject matter* of conceptual enquiry, not language as such. Summers included the following on an "inexhaustive" list of concepts studied by conceptual analysts: concepts used in formulating theories of law (e.g., sources of law, adjudication, minimum efficacy, sanctions); concepts that are more or less creatures of law (e.g., ownership, corporation); concepts used in formulations of substantive laws (e.g., intention, causation, possession); and concepts used to demarcate basic legal relations (e.g., right-duty, power-liability). The family of activities involved in "analysis", according to Summers, included breaking down concepts, differentiating related concepts, correlating and/or unifying related concepts, classifying them in some way and charting their implications.

With the benefit of Summers' comments we can begin to address the question, "at what level of analysis is conceptual analysis of the kind practised by jurists such as Hart compatible with Weberian sociology"? The answer almost certainly lies in an equally weighted but discriminating *combination* of the tasks identified above: (i) analyses of existing conceptual frameworks for law; and (ii) use of newly constructed frameworks, such as (for example) Hart's nucleic expository theory. The parameters of the sociological and juristic assignments suggested by Weber are provisionally set in his sociological point of view. The normative conceptions embedded in the subjective meaning of relevant law-affected behaviour (including, but not limited to, the behaviour of those who exercise significant power) are causes or consequences of certain regularities. The interpretive and causal aspects of Weberian sociological enquiry are present here. Where there may be *incompatibility* is where *entire* "newly constructed" frameworks simply do not fit within the parameters of the sociological point of view. Without doubt, *aspects* of such frameworks may be selectively liberated from their background to shed light upon underlying normative conceptions. In addition, there is the further prospect of applying the main analytical activities which Summers identifies: breaking down, differentiating and classifying concepts—such as adjudication, efficacy, sanctions, legal relations and so on—and correlating and/or unifying related concepts. In pursuing those tasks it is again useful to draw upon insights of the analytical tradition. For that purpose, however, it is not essential to focus exclusively upon Hart. Jurists such as Hohfeld may justifiably enter the picture.

Causality in the Sociological Point of View

I have briefly considered the conceptual aspect of the sociological point of view. In the context of Weberian sociology, an equally important aspect is *causality*. It is useful for a moment to examine just where causality fits into this viewpoint. In focusing on what *actually* happens owing to the probability that individuals orient their social action by reference to legal norms, law is seen as being in some sense causative of empirical regularities in the world of human behaviour. In his essay, "The Concept of 'Following a Rule'", Weber discusses the hypothesis of a worker who comes to rely on the "chance" of periodically receiving "certain metal discs" or "pieces of paper" (money) in return for performing certain services, and who knows that this money can be exchanged for "bread, cabbages, trousers and so on".[16] He knows, moreover, that "if anyone thereafter tries to take these objects away from him again, there is a certain probability that men with spiked helmets will appear in response to his cries for help and will assist him to regain possession of them".

For Weber, the fact that the factory owner can rely on the probability that the worker will perform services—and, by extension, that the worker can rely on the probability that money will be accepted in exchange for goods, all of which is, in a sense, "guaranteed" by coercive agencies—involves "causal conditions of a certain 'technical' outcome". In a logical sense, according to Weber, these causal conditions are no different because "conscious processes" are inserted into the causal chain—i.e., the act of thought which

---

[16] Max Weber, "The Concept of 'Following a Rule'", in W G Runciman (ed.), *Max Weber, Selections in Translation* (Cambridge University Press, 1978), ch. 5, esp. 101.

is "co-operation according to rules"—than similar causal conditions found in other situations, such as Weber's example: that the formation of x tonnes of pig iron will result from the use of y tonnes of ore in space z. This example is characteristic of "concrete reality" in the sense of *Naturwissenschaften*. According to Weber, the rules to which the factory owner, worker and countless others orient their behaviour are "maxims" which causally affect the empirical behaviour of individuals, and which are "rules" in the causal sense which have been acquired by reasoned experience or learned from others, of the type, "If I do x, in accordance with empirical rules, y will result". Weber concludes that the actor has to calculate, in the light of experience, the mode of reaction of the "external world" to certain modes of his or her own behaviour. It makes no difference to the "logical" character of these "maxims" that in the one case they include human reactions, while in the other they include only reactions by animals, plants and "inanimate" natural objects.

Crucially, however, the norms or maxims of behaviour, when they are considered by Weber to be "causes" or determinants of human action, are "causes" purely in an empirical sense, the point being that the investigator can only have knowledge of the content of the mind of another individual through the empirical, externally observable manifestation of what is known only to that other individual. The following of a norm, by conscious orientation of behaviour by reference to that norm, is "empirical" and "causal" in a unique sense. As Weber says:[17]

"When . . . it is said that the rule in question, whether moral, conventional or teleological, is the 'cause' of a certain action, this is of course an extremely imprecise way of putting it: it is not the 'ideal validity' of a norm, but the empirical representation in the mind of an agent that the norm 'ought to be applied' in his behaviour which is the cause."

The representation of (say) a legal norm in the mind of an actor is something observable only in outward manifestations of speech or other medium. If action is in some way modified in consequence of the existence of the norm, that too is observable. The observer

[17] Ibid., 105.

can apply knowledge of meaningful behaviour—for example, that by and large behaviour may be influenced by norms—by conferring meaning on manifestations of mental content. The meaning so conferred may be combined with the purely empirical observation of the constant conjunction or regular sequence of "events": i.e., one event following another.

Official (particularly judicial) behaviour may be looked upon as being at least in theory capable of analysis into "events" which stand in causal relationships to one another, but only to the extent that causal imputation lends itself to such analysis, to a greater or lesser degree of success. It hardly matters that in a practical sense such behaviour consists of a continuous stream of "events", each of which, taken with other "events", is at any given time capable of being analysed as a "preceding event" in relation to a "supervening event" and a "supervening event" in relation to a "preceding event". The observer may be content to look at a course of behaviour as a whole rather than attempt to break down and individuate all of the elements of particular sequences of events.

Hart and the Role of the Jurist

Hart's failure to attempt to outline a coherent role for the jurist in *The Concept of Law* is significant. The importance of Weber's sociological point of view is that it sets rudimentary terms of reference for sociological enquiry into law. Not all sociologists of law would subscribe to a programme directed towards an examination of what "actually happens" owing to a "probability" that individuals—with the emphasis on those holding office in political or legal institutions—orient their social (official) action by reference to legal norms. Moreover, the analysis of underlying legal conceptions, particularly in the manner of twentieth century analytical jurisprudence, may not feature high on the list of priorities of many sociologists of law. Yet Weber's terms of reference are highly functional as a commencement point for a basically "syncretic", or integrationist, approach to theoretical enquiry into law. It is "integrationist" in the sense that Weberian sociology is the relevant frame of reference. Conceptual analysis and other modes of enquiry, such as those identified by Summers, may be integrated into that (wider) context. The sociological point of view at the same time defines a *role*: that of the "jurisprudentially sensitive" social scientific investigator. That role can be developed towards that of the social scientist *versed in* jurisprudential conceptual analysis or debates within traditional jurisprudence. The jurist acting in the role of Weberian social scientist, then, may adopt Weber's sociological point of view, or some constructively elaborated variant of that viewpoint that draws upon the techniques of interpretive understanding and causal imputation as well as the postulates of value-relation and value-freedom. To the extent that the social scientistic jurist is also a *legal positivist*, the object of enquiry is law as "posited" or created by human act of will. The techniques of conceptual analysis which are so characteristic of twentieth century analytical jurisprudence are also highly important as I, and others, have argued.

Iudex as an ideal type

One of the consequences of Weber's epistemological stance against the neo-Kantians of the Southwest German School was his adoption of the view that social science as a nomothetic—as opposed to idiographic—discipline could validly evolve a methodology in which abstraction and the formation of sociological concepts were a key to knowledge of the world of human behaviour. Weber observes, in *Economy and Society*,[18] that "the science of sociology seeks to formulate type concepts and generalized uniformities of empirical process. This distinguishes it from history, which is oriented to the causal analysis and explanation of individual actions, structures, and personalities possessing cultural significance". Critics of Weber have argued that his position in relation to the neo-Kantians—who included Wilhelm Windelband, Heinrich Rickert and Emil Lask—was neither unproblematic nor free from contradiction. One commentator has concluded that Weber failed to grasp some of Rickert's most important arguments in *Die Grenzen der naturwissenschaftlichen Begriffsbildung*—Rickert's major work.[19] The entire

[18] Max Weber, *The Theory of Social and Economic Organization* (The Free Press, New York, 1947) (*TSEO*), 109.

[19] See Guy Oakes, "Weber and the Southwest German School: The Genesis of the Concept of the Historical Individual", in Wolfgang J Mommsen and

area of concept formation in social science was fraught with difficulty, controversy and esotericism in Weber's time, to say nothing of later scholarly developments.

It is beyond the scope of this book to engage with these debates. The attempt to formulate a rudimentary model of an imaginary ultimate judge proceeds from the standpoint that however much Weberian social science may inform, or provide a context for, the development of such a model, its explanatory power will succeed or fail less on the basis of its social theory content than of its juristic content. Indeed, so extensive is relevant literature that even a scholarly work devoted strictly to the *jurisprudence* of adjudication and the judicial role may be hard pressed to do justice to that subject matter. *A fortiori* a piece of interdisciplinary writing may defensibly limit itself to attempting the clearest *outline* of the relevant subject area compatible with reasonable fulfilment of stated objectives. The analytical construct *Iudex* to be outlined in skeleton form in this chapter is purely a heuristic device: a viewpoint theoretically conceived for the purpose of clarifying how legal meaning in a sense to be discussed comes to be ascribed. The task of formulating such a device is intended, moreover, to go some way towards explicitly supplying an institutional insider's viewpoint from which legal relationships may be imagined to emanate. Hart's failure in this respect resulted in his uncritically presenting a concept of law essentially from an insider's point of view (to the apparent exclusion of other valid viewpoints) either: from the "internal" point of view of a citizenry who, by and large, "accept" the law as expressed in primary rules; or from the "internal" point of view of judges and other officials who "accept" the law as expressed in secondary rules.

The Weberian Ideal Type Revisited

A few reiterative comments on the Weberian concept of the ideal type may serve to place *Iudex* in an appropriate theoretical context. Weber's doctrine of *Wertbeziehung* (value-relevance) entailed that values which incorporate criteria of significance enable the investigator to make a selection from the inexhaustible plurality of possible objects of cognition. Weber held that the investigator was in the

Jürgen Osterhammel (eds.), *Max Weber and his Contemporaries* (The German Historical Institute) (Allen & Unwin, London, 1987), 434 at 444.

best position to assess significance, influenced by the nature of the problems being investigated, the subject matter and the particular questions standing in need of resolution. Relevant values were thus to be selected and adopted *by the investigator*. Following through that approach, an ideal type was formed by a synthesis of concrete individual phenomena arranged according to "one-sidedly emphasized viewpoints" into a unified analytical construct. A given type of action could be characterised in terms of theoretically conceived subjective meanings attributed to hypothetical actors. The ideal type incorporated similarities found in a multiplicity of typical cases not necessarily corresponding to any specific actors. At any rate, to concentrate on the unique attributes of particular individuals would tend to negate the rationale of type formulation through abstraction.

A few key aspects of the judicial role may now be outlined using Weber's ideal type methodology. At the outset, a sociologically inclined jurist may, by extension, be substituted for Weber's "investigator". The judicial role to be outlined hypothesises a hierarchically ultimate judge of an imaginary Euro-American type legal system, i.e., a judge sitting in a final court of appeal. Why, specifically, is *judicial* social action worthy of typification? In at least one of its manifestations, "law" may be understood in the sense of Weber's concept of "guaranteed law". In that sense there exists a "coercive apparatus" consisting of "one or more persons whose special task it is to hold themselves ready to apply specially provided means of coercion (legal coercion) for the purpose of norm enforcement".[20] A focus of sociological interest has been suggested earlier in this chapter in Weber's words: "[T]he legal guarantees and their underlying normative conceptions are of interest both as consequences and as causes or concomitant causes of certain regularities of human action . . . or of regularities of natural occurrences engendered by human action . . .".[21] It is a fact that much human

---

[20] *ES*, 313; *LES*, 13. Weber also makes reference to the concept of the "legal order": "A 'legal order' shall . . . be said to exist wherever coercive means, of a physical or psychological kind, are available; i.e., wherever they are at the disposal of one or more persons who hold themselves ready to use them for this purpose in the case of certain events; in other words, wherever we find a consociation specifically dedicated to the purpose of 'legal coercion' ". (*ES*, 317).

[21] *ES*, 332; *LES*, 34.

behaviour follows causal regularities not only because action is oriented by reference to legal norms and normative conceptions but because special coercive apparatuses exist which, under appropriate conditions, take action to ensure compliance with, or to apply sanctions in response to violations of, legal norms. As I will argue in chapter 6, it is part of the adjudicatory function—the function of legal institutions which include courts and tribunals—to confer evaluative meaning upon relevant factual states of affairs by reference to applicable legal norms and other normative conceptions. On the basis of such ascriptions of legal meaning, relevant coercive apparatuses are mobilised to take official enforcement action. Those apparatuses—which exercise significant social power—as I have mentioned, are thus kept in check by an interposing mechanism of courts and tribunals. Adjudication as a specific type of social action is of interest to the sociologically inclined jurist because it is part of the process that regulates the use and exercise of that power.

Our first assumption, then, is of a hypothetical judge (treated as "ego"), who orients his or her official action partly by reference to the evaluative meaning which he or she ascribes to perceived states of "fact" (e.g., human behaviour) attributable to one or more others (treated as "alter"). The "others" in question may, for example, be litigants or persons otherwise involved in legal proceedings. This ascribed meaning is the legal meaning of the states of affairs in question: that is, the meaning which such states of affairs bear by reference to legal norms. (I will give more detailed consideration to the notion of legal meaning, and to the evaluative, orientative and regulatory functions of norms, in chapter 6.) A key aspect of this interpretive process is the activity of conceiving of the position of litigants—or other parties involved in the process—in relational terms, i.e., in terms of rights, duties, powers or liabilities. These conceptual acts are at the centre of judicial interpretive processes but are only *part*, albeit an important part, of the specialised activity of adjudication. Again, a more detailed discussion of relationality follows in chapters 6 and 7.

Adjudication involves making judgments about human action or events attributed to human intervention. But judges do not, though they often may, simply and mechanically declare (for instance) that one litigant stands in a specified relationship with respect to another litigant. The act of ascribing legal relationships is by no means a mechanical process since adjudication utilises an array of conceptual techniques. Even in the case of relatively straightforward legal disputes—so-called "hard cases" aside[22]—the ascriptive act may be as much constitutive as it is declaratory of legal relationships. In a civil action, for example, the operation of adjective legal norms may operate to "transform" one litigant's substantive claim against another into a type of "claim" against the court for a remedy.

The performative act ordered by the court may be qualitatively different from that prescribed by relevant substantive norms. For instance a contractual "performance obligation" (e.g., to construct a road) may be converted through breach of contract into a payment obligation: a requirement to pay damages. Also, a court may place a nuance of meaning on substantive norms which litigants had not contemplated at any prior stage despite the fact that until the matter goes to court the litigants have acted in some respect in accordance with their own (non-authoritative) interpretation. Substantive claims of civil litigants as conceived from their own point of view are seldom left "intact" following adjudication because compromises must be made, interests must be weighed and balanced, and competing interpretations of legal norms and of factual events to which legal meaning is ascribed must be resolved in favour of one or other party. Furthermore, the court's power to classify or reclassify legally relevant "facts" for legal purposes by reference to legal norms may result in the constitution anew of legal relationships between civil litigants.

Regularities that proceed from the activity of adjudication—flowing specifically from a hierarchically ultimate level—have been mentioned briefly. Now *because* judicial action mobilises coercive and sanction-exacting forces in society, countless individuals, in attempting to imagine the legal consequences of their action and that of others "out of court" (to use Hart's phrase), may strive to adopt the same perspective as an "ultimate judge". In this way an individual may attempt to visualise what the legal result would be

---

[22] See Ronald Dworkin's discussion of "hard cases", in *Taking Rights Seriously* (Fifth Impression) (Gerald Duckworth & Co. Ltd., 1977), ch. 4 at 81 *et seq.*

of a given course of action, or of *any* legally relevant "facts", based on the hypothesis of what the legal result would be *if* a dispute were to arise or criminal proceedings were to be brought following the occurrence of certain "events" and this dispute or those proceedings were to be litigated or tried to a point in the system where a final and authoritative determination was made. In other words, what would be the rights, duties, powers and liabilities of the litigants or, as the case may be, criminal suspects? It may become part of the legal culture of a society for individuals—who may include private citizens, court or prison officials, lawyers, police officers, accountants, tax inspectors, and so on—to act on such a hypothesis. Legal training may come to be structured around it. Questions set in university examination papers take for granted that the "best" legal authority—legal precedents established in higher courts of law, if not the highest court—will be cited in support of propositions of law. Private individuals, either by themselves or, more usually, with the assistance of legally qualified professionals, often seek to employ the same techniques of "fact-finding" and legal reasoning employed throughout and at the highest hierarchical level of a legal system. In the context (say) of English law it would be pointless to follow a legal principle established at the level of a lower court when a principle on precisely the same point, established at the level of the House of Lords, *differs* from the lower court's principle. Unquestionably, behavioural regularities on a far-reaching scale result from the fact that action is oriented broadly in accordance with such imagined, hypothetical legal outcomes. The hypothesis of the ultimate judgment proceeds from the viewpoint of the ultimate judge, *Iudex*. It is to more particular aspects of that imaginary viewpoint that we now turn our attention.

The Concept of the Office

The typical judge of a western legal system—for example, a legal system on the Euro-American model—is, in effect, a role-occupant who discharges functions to which certain duties are attached. These determine the tasks, actions and behaviours associated with the position which the official is expected—and which he or she may feel more or less bound—to perform. The position itself is called an *office*. *Iudex* may be taken to be the hypothetical holder of

103

judicial office at the highest—i.e., supreme, or highest appeal court—level of the legal system of a hypothetical western-type state. Weber gives a classic account of the main features of the concept of office in his ideal typification of bureaucracy.[23] He analyses office as a role to which expected functions attach which are in some sense detached from the individual occupying the office. Those functions subsist notwithstanding a change in the individual occupying the office at any given time. The "identity" attaching to the office as such—e.g., the office of president—is independent of the identity of the occupant in his or her individual capacity. An office usually functions as a component of a formal organisation.

According to Weber, the typical person in authority occupying an office is subject to an impersonal order towards which his or her actions are oriented. This is true not only for persons exercising legal authority, but "for the elected president of a state". Anyone obeying an official in authority owes obedience to the impersonal order rather than to the person as an individual. The separation of the official's individual and official capacities is also reflected in the separation of property belonging to the organisation and the personal property of the official. The office does not vest in the official personally and it is not normally in the gift of the official to transfer the office to another party, though often an official may delegate authority.

The specialised training necessary to qualify someone for occupancy of an office restricts the candidature for the position to a circle of persons holding relevant qualifications. Within that circle, a principle of successive replaceability may apply in that one incumbent can always be replaced by another holding similar qualifications. The possession of unusual skills by a candidate may be a desirable, though not necessary, qualification for holding office. Rational legal authority confers on officials what Weber calls a "specified sphere of competence". The obligation to obey an official applies only within the sphere of the rationally delimited authority conferred upon the official. This sphere of competence involves:[24]

[23] *TSEO*, 302 *et seq*. See also Robert Bierstedt, *The Social Order* (Tata McGraw-Hill Publishing Co. Ltd., 3rd ed. 1970), 249. See further Robert K Merton, *Social Theory and Social Structure* (The Free Press, New York, 1957), 195.

[24] *TSEO*, 330.

". . . (a) a sphere of obligations to perform functions which has been marked off as part of a systematic division of labour. (b) The provision of the incumbent with the necessary authority to carry out these functions. (c) That the necessary means of compulsion are clearly defined and their use is subject to definite conditions."

The three characteristics of the office outlined above—separation of official from individual identity, successive replaceability and conferment of a specified sphere of competence—impact upon the nature of law as an institutionally ascriptive activity (to be discussed in chapter 6 below). A sphere of competence establishes the nature of the activities entailed in the execution of the office. At the same time the office sharply differentiates between the individual and official capacities of the occupant. In the *ideal* case the judge acting as functionary may be looked upon as one whose conception of substantive legal relationships—e.g., a right/duty relationship subsisting between litigants—is shaped by requirements imposed by the office and not by considerations personal to the judge as an individual. An element of judicial discretion is not necessarily inconsistent with the adoption of an "official line", though unbridled creativity may not generally be regarded as part of the role of the "ideal" judge. The judicial creativity of "non-ideal" judges—assuming that creativity is excluded from the ideal role—may be seen as a deviation from the ideal type. The principles of identity separation and successive replaceability ensure that an ideal judge—transcending, in a sense, his or her own individuality—establishes a pattern of judicial activity which is not given to arbitrariness or caprice. In other words, unless an exercise of judicial discretion is called for in a particular case the judge's personal identity will not *normally* make any practical difference to the outcome of the case. The criteria for selection of candidates for judicial office may reinforce uniformity by eliminating those who would be unlikely to discharge the duties of the office in accordance with its acknowledged terms of reference.

In this idealised setting, the ascription of a substantive legal relationship—an ascription of legal meaning at the substantive level—is not an "emanation" from an individual in any accepted sense. It is, rather, the product of, or an "emanation" from, an essentially synthetic persona—the holder of judicial office. *Ex hypothesi* this persona conceives legal relationships through the filter of officially posited criteria. The fact that judges must act within a "sphere of competence" entails that many official acts are "duty acts" in the sense of acts complying with norms determining what may or may not lawfully be done. As we have seen, Hart refers to these norms as rules of adjudication. The *ideal-typical* judge occupying an office may thus be seen largely as an instrument of the impersonal order within which he or she operates.

Adjudication

As a type of social action, the activity of judging human behaviour—that of adjudication—involves taking account of the behaviour of others in a special way. The normal context in which recourse to adjudication is appropriate is a situation in which at least two parties are in dispute regarding some matter. This implies a civil law dispute. At least one of the parties may wish the dispute to be resolved by means of the *judgment* or decision of a designated person—i.e., a judge or other official. Where a crime has been committed, criminal proceedings are appropriate. In that situation the parties involved are, on the one hand, a criminal suspect and, on the other hand, a private or public prosecutor. The adjudicatory function involves a kind of intervention in the governance of the relationships between one human being (or entity) and another. According to this simplifying account, adjudication fulfils its function of settling disputes by making use of a technique in which human relationships are conceived as relationships whose content is defined by legal norms. In practice—and considerably simplified—this technique involves three processes:

1. the ascertainment of "facts" considered relevant in the context of the adjudication;
2. the ascertainment by processes of law-finding or law-creation of legal norms considered relevant in the context of the adjudication;
3. the "application" of the legal norms so ascertained to the "facts" so ascertained.

The first two activities—ascertainment of "facts" and of legal norms—are essential preliminaries to the third activity: the "application" of legal norms to "facts". This third activity involves the ascription of legal meaning which enters into the subjective meaning of official judicial action. In the present context legal meaning is to be seen in terms of the hypothesis of the subjective meaning of the official action of *Iudex*. Legal relationships are conceived, conclusively and authoritatively, by *Iudex*. *Iudex*'s official action is oriented to the effect of issuing a judgment, sentence or other enforcement order. The third activity mentioned above is, in a sense, the end of adjudication: the determination of the content of legal relationships obtaining between litigants or other interested parties. Adjudication is thus primarily concerned with the ascertainment for legal purposes of the content of rights, duties, powers, liabilities or other legal relationships.

A jurist who may be seen as pivotal between a sociological notion of subjective meaning (*Sinn*) and the notion of meaning in legal theory is Hans Kelsen. We have seen in chapter 1 that Kelsen used the expression *legal meaning* (*rechtliche Bedeutung*), though not in any overtly "sociological" sense. In holding that legal science belonged to the human sciences, Kelsen was already some way towards acknowledging the influence of the German *Geisteswissenschaften* approach to the social world. In the *Pure Theory of Law*[25] he comments that a social act can carry with it an indication of its own meaning. In any event, Kelsen did not deny the social nature of the legal world: "Law is a social phenomenon, that is, observable in society . . .".[26] Kelsen recognises that actors attach a definite meaning to an act expressed "in some fashion or other and which is understood by those towards whom the act is directed".[27] The notion that meaning is capable of

[25] Above at n. 5.

[26] *PTL*, 8.

[27] Kelsen comments: "This is a special characteristic of the material dealt with in social and in particular in juristic knowledge. A plant can convey nothing about itself to the research worker who is trying to define it. It makes no attempt to explain itself scientifically. But a social act can very well carry with it an indication of its own meaning". See Hans Kelsen, "The Pure Theory of Law" (1934) 50 *Law Quarterly Review* at 478, 480–1. See also Hans Kelsen, *Pure Theory of Law* (University of California Press, Berkeley and Los Angeles, 2nd ed. 1967), 2–3. Compare Weber's observation: "[In sociological analysis we] . . . can accomplish something which is never attainable in the natural sciences; namely the subjective understanding of the action of the component

attachment to human acts both by the actor and by others towards whom the act is directed is fashioned by Kelsen into a more specific conception of *legally* meaningful phenomena: especially "acts" or "events" or "facts".[28] Kelsen, too, acknowledges that the legal meaning of facts—the "objective meaning", as Kelsen describes it—may not coincide with the subjective meaning, i.e., the meaning from the point of view of a private individual:[29]

> "The legal meaning of an act, as an external fact, is not immediately perceptible by the senses. . . . This subjective meaning may, but need not necessarily, coincide with its objective meaning, that is, the meaning the act has according to the law. For example, somebody makes some dispositions, stating in writing what is to happen to his belongings when he dies. The subjective meaning of this act is a testament. Objectively, however, it is not, because some legal formalities were not observed."

Legal norms themselves are presented as the meaning of certain "acts of will": law-creating acts of will.[30] Kelsen advances a conception of the legal norm as a "scheme of interpretation" at various points in different texts. In essence, every legal or illegal act has a specifically legal meaning. The content of a relevant legal norm refers to the act so that the act is capable of interpretation by reference to the norm. The conceptual act of interpretation is, for Kelsen, a "thinking process" involving "confrontation" of the relevant act with a relevant norm.

---

individuals. The natural sciences on the other hand cannot do this, being limited to the formulation of causal uniformities in objects and events and the explanation of individual facts by applying them. We do not 'understand' the behaviour of cells, but can only observe the relevant functional relationships and generalize on the basis of these observations" (*TSEO*, 103–4).

[28] See Hans Kelsen, *Pure Theory of Law* above at n. 27, 2–5.

[29] Ibid., 2–3.

[30] As Kelsen comments: " 'Norm' is the meaning of an act by which a certain behavior is commanded, permitted, or authorized. The norm, as the specific meaning of an act directed toward the behavior of someone else, is to be carefully differentiated from the act of will whose meaning the norm is: the norm is an *ought*, but the act of will is an *is*" (*Pure Theory of Law* above at n. 27, 5). See also Bernard S Jackson, *Semiotics and Legal Theory* (Routledge & Kegan Paul, London, 1985), 227–8 and 229 *et seq.*

Adjudication, then, is first a process concerned with the ascertainment and interpretation of "facts" that are relevant to the subject matter of the adjudication. It is for the court to ascertain any issues in dispute between the parties and to reach a determination, usually in favour of one party against the other. The determination of "facts" in the legal sense through an evidence-adducing process is an integral part of this activity.

Hohfeld views "operative facts" as legally relevant "facts" whose occurrence triggers the operation of a legal norm. In the present context this would give grounds for the ascription by *Iudex* of a legal relationship to appropriate legal persons. The problem of selecting "facts" out of the limitless flux of everyday life is addressed from a practical point of view by a test of relevancy applied to the legal norms bearing on the issues before the court and by a test of relevancy and materiality of "facts". The latter test involves the evaluation of facts by reference to appropriate value criteria. That process filters out "facts" considered relatively trivial, and at the same time gives prominence to "facts" considered material.

Where a division of labour—such as that between judge and jury—exists within a legal system the hypothetical judgment of *Iudex*—which is taken to be the "ultimate" judgment of the system—is no less the judgment of *Iudex* because those at a lower level in the hierarchy have made decisions (e.g. as to findings of fact) that are treated for legal purposes as conclusive both for that and for superior levels in the hierarchy. The act of hypothesising the judgment of an ideal type such as *Iudex* in a sense involves a willing suspension of disbelief. It requires recognition of the procedural reality of a legal hierarchy in which "ultimate" judgments are themselves composites or syntheses of *many* decisions and findings of law and "fact" taken at different levels in the adjudication process. In theoretical terms, an element of the *Iudexian* judgment must reflect the artificial rules of a legal system whereby the actual judgment of a supreme court is a synthesis of the action—decisions, judgments, findings, and so on—of numerous actors within the adjudicatory process.

It is not at all clear whether the second activity associated with adjudication—ascertainment of relevant legal norms—follows or precedes the process of ascertaining relevant "facts", since both processes are often inextricable. The question of which legal rule or principle may be applicable in a given case may depend on knowledge of material facts. But, on the other hand, the materiality of facts may be predetermined by relevant legal rules or principles, whether these be rules of evidence or substantive rules or principles. On a practical level the applicability of legal norms may be guided in some sense by the perceived occurrence of material "facts". On a theoretical level, legal positivism has given primacy to the notion of *legal validity* as specifying criteria for determining whether a norm is a *legal* norm to be applied in the context of a specific case. On one view, legal validity refers to that quality—such as "origin"— which attaches or is attributed to an individual norm and which determines more or less conclusively whether it is to be treated as belonging to a given legal system. A norm so designated is treated as one by reference to which the personnel of the legal system evaluate and orient their official action and evaluate the behaviour of others—e.g., litigants—with a view to the orientation of their official action.

Hart's rule of recognition is a criterion of legal validity in the sense of the present discussion. There must be some means by which legal personnel may conclusively identify what is to count as a valid norm of a particular system to enable coercive apparatuses (ultimately) to be mobilised to take official enforcement action. Factual identificatory criteria are a necessary part of legal processes. Such criteria could, perhaps, be regarded as being *incorporated within* a legal norm, such as Hart's rule of adjudication, or could take other forms. Superficially, recognition criteria reside in propositions such as "a document of description X is a statute", "a casebook of description Y contains judgments of the court of appeal", and so on. Recognition criteria may furthermore require that certain procedural formalities be satisfied in relation to specific types of law: for example, that a statute or bye-law has been duly "passed" or otherwise promulgated in accordance with a specified procedure.

The third major activity involved in adjudication—that of "applying" legal norms to "facts"—is fundamental to the technique of ascribing legal relationships. The rights and duties of litigants are authoritatively expressed in the form of the court's judgment. For

Kelsen, an essential feature of the judicial decision-making process is that factual conditions conceived *in abstracto* under the generalising terms of a legal norm must be found to be present *in concreto*: in the "actuality" of the case presented to the court.[31] Kelsen argues that this involves the creation of an individual norm which addresses the specific facts of the individual case. The general norm is "concretised" in its application to "reality": "The general norm which, to certain abstractly determined conditions, attaches certain abstractly determined consequences, has to be individualised and concretised in order to come in contact with social life, to be applied to reality".[32]

Law-application also has causal significance in that the coercive apparatuses of the legal order are set in motion conditionally upon the finding, articulation and ascription by a court of rights, duties and other legal relationships at the substantive level. Hypothetically, *Iudex* occupies a position on the causal and temporal continuum that has its origin in the perceived occurrence of "operative facts" and its resolution in the enforcement action which follows upon the judgment of—if necessary—a final court of appeal. In a sense, *Iudex* is involved, though not necessarily actively, at all points on this continuum. first, evidence tending to establish the prior occurrence of "operative facts", using Hohfeld's expression, is presented to the court. Secondly, the court is involved in assessing the procedural validity of lawsuit-instituting "events" and other procedural steps attending the initiation of legal proceedings and conduct of the case. Thirdly, the court itself issues a "judgment". And, fourthly, this "judgment" under certain conditions constitutes a basis for the orientation of the official action of "coercive agencies" such as the police or prison officers. To the extent, if at all, that each "event" on this causal continuum is capable of individuation, it is possible to imagine a sequential progression in which one "event" is seen to lead inevitably to another (later) "event". Such a progression is at least envisaged by Weber's causal rendition of the legal right in which there exists a probability that an individual—a natural or

---

[31] Hans Kelsen, *General Theory of Law and State* (Russell & Russell, New York, 1961), 135.
[32] Ibid.

juridical person—may invoke the aid of a "coercive apparatus" for the enforcement of his, her or its legal right. In theory *Iudex* ascribes legal meaning to each component "event".

It is for the investigator—the sociologically inclined jurist—to attain an understanding of judicial (institutional) meaning in general and to reformulate this in terms of the *Iudexian* ideal type. As mutually verifying processes the Weberian investigator examines whether the meaning to be incorporated into the *Iudexian* type construct is supported by the causal regularities observed, and, correspondingly, whether those "external facts" are borne out by the investigator's interpretive hypotheses. The interpretive and causal explanations of judicial social action thus find their expression in the ideal type construct *Iudex* in terms that the judgment of a court is to be seen not merely as something meaningful in its own right and a product of "events" (e.g., "operative facts") to which meaning has been ascribed, but may also be seen as at least a likely outcome of certain conditioning "events" (such as "operative facts") and thus as an "event" itself which is capable more or less of determination in terms of probability. The judgment of a court may be causally and interpretively significant beyond the immediate range of parties directly affected by it, i.e., beyond litigants and officials concerned with enforcement. As a legal precedent the decision may be a basis for orientation of future action of officials and numerous others. Strictly speaking, those causal regularities lie beyond the scope of an ideal-type construct concerned more narrowly with an explanation of judicial action. But their causal and interpretive significance should not be underestimated.

Ultimacy

The final aspect of the Weberian judicial ideal type construct to be briefly considered is *ultimacy*. It is as much a practical as a rational requirement that a system of adjudication, however rudimentary, should be so organised that at one or more stages in the process it is capable of yielding a determination which, for purposes of the system, conclusively establishes or disposes of an issue of law or "fact"—or one combining law and "fact"—that is the subject of civil litigation or criminal proceedings. From a practical point of view the system would break down if every "finding" of "fact", interpretation of law and "application" of law to "fact" were perpetually open to reconsideration. There could be no faith in the certainty of the decision-making processes of such a system. Furthermore, litigants would be unable to act in reliance upon judgments made by a court at any given time. A precedent-based system of adjudication that permitted the perpetual reopening of cases for reconsideration would surely generate a meaningless collection of inconsistent and contradictory decisions which could not constitute a secure basis for the orientation of social action.

A hierarchical structure of adjudication normally makes provision for certain elements of an issue in dispute—usually "findings" of "fact"—to be disposed of at a designated level of the hierarchy which is generally non-ultimate. Other elements—usually determinations of law or "applications" of law to "fact"—may, in general, be conclusively disposed of only at the highest or ultimate hierarchical level. The system's final and authoritative declaration of the legal relationships obtaining between litigants, or between prosecutor and accused, is treated for all purposes as incapable of appeal to any further level of the hierarchy because there is no other (i.e., superior) level. The existence of this Hohfeldian "disability"—or "no-power" to pursue the issue further—establishes the finality of the system's determination. In some systems of adjudication a principle of finality is enshrined in the doctrine of *res judicata* in terms of which a judgment that has been appealed to an ultimate hierarchical level exhausts the merits of the issue in dispute. Such a judgment may not normally be subject to further review.

The principle of finality correspondingly enters the construct *Iudex* whose position at the ultimate level of the adjudicatory hierarchy ensures the finality of the *Iudexian* judgment. Adjudicatory ultimacy is a concomitant of hierarchical ultimacy. Finality and authoritativeness are theoretically attributed to *Iudex's* official role. It is also to be assumed that every "ultimate judgment" is exclusively attributable to *Iudex*, though the judgment may, in practical terms, incorporate a series of other decisions, interpretations of law or "findings" of "fact" established at prior stages in the adjudication process. A judicial act—a judgment—attributed to *Iudex* may thus be treated for *theoretical* purposes as constituting a definitive statement of the legal relationships of parties to legal proceedings, at least in so far as the mobilisation of the coercive apparatuses of the legal system is concerned. It does not follow, however, that such judicial acts constitute a definitive statement of the "legally correct" decision. It is beyond the scope of the present discussion to consider that issue, however. Suffice it to say that "legal correctness" and "legal authoritativeness" are not necessarily co-extensive.

The official world view

Iudex is a theoretically conceived viewpoint formulated primarily to highlight the distinctive institutional perspective from which legally relevant behaviour and other factual events may—for theoretical purposes—be perceived. *Iudex* is thus a heuristic device aimed at clarifying aspects of the institutionally ascriptive nature of state law. Ascription in that sense is further examined in chapter 6 below. The perspective of any *actual* judge—still less a theoretical construct such as *Iudex*—is not the only, nor necessarily the most important, point of view from which law may be perceived or critically evaluated. Donald Galloway's accusation of conservatism against Hart might be thought to apply to a perspective such as that of *Iudex* if the reader—like the chastened linguistic philosopher whom Galloway caricatures—is "passively led" by such a perspective "into 'the official reality', without the thought of illusion or mirage entering his head".[33] The *Iudexian* viewpoint is intended to be seen merely as a counterpoint to *other* viewpoints, however. There is nothing to prevent a conception of the world as it happens to be to, for instance, a marginalised indigenous community being expressed through that community's world view and given the scrutiny afforded by an appropriate methodology. Such a conception—existing alongside a theoretically constructed institutional viewpoint—may throw into relief the "gap" between those viewpoints. Although it is beyond the scope of this book to examine specific contrasting viewpoints, the *possibility* of doing so is deserving of further comment. I will revisit that possibility briefly at the end of chapter 8.

[33] See Donald Galloway, "The Axiology of Analytical Jurisprudence: A Study of the Underlying Sociological Assumptions and Ideological Predilections", in Thomas W Bechtler (ed.), *Law in a Social Context: Liber Amicorum Honouring Professor Lon L. Fuller* (Kluwer, The Netherlands, 1978) 74.

We have also seen that a definition of the viewpoint and theoretical orientation of the jurist may impact significantly on the nature and direction of theoretical tasks such as—but not confined to—the formulation of a perspective such as that of *Iudex*. Another important task, suggested by Weber's sociological point of view, is the examination of legal guarantees and their underlying normative conceptions as causes or consequences of observable behavioural regularities. In chapters 6 and 7—in the course of tackling the Second and Third Gordian Knots—I will consider in more detail such "normative conceptions", focusing, in particular, on the nature and structure of legal relationships, or "jural relations" as Hohfeld refers to them.

6
"Reductionism" Reassessed

"A normative orientation is fundamental to the schema of action in the same sense that space is fundamental to that of the classical mechanics: in terms of the given conceptual scheme there is no such thing as action except as effort to conform with norms just as there is no such thing as motion except as change of location in space." *Talcott Parsons*[1]

The second Gordian Knot revisited

The problem of "reductionism" to legal "rules", highlighted under the Second Gordian Knot, was fundamental. It is a problem that, in a variety of subtle ways, produced theoretical distortion or obscured alternative ways of perceiving law that were potentially quite revealing. I argued that the problem of "reductionism" was manifested in the following way. The reduction of human behaviour, activities, social action, and so on, to legal "rules" denied the possibility of giving equal weight to normative *and behavioural* aspects of the legal world. The possibility of viewing law as complexes of activities—specific institutional activities which *only to an extent* are rule-governed—was de-emphasised. In cases where a legal system was equated to a *system of rules*, or the object of theoretical enquiry was exclusively focused upon rules, an entire dimension of the legal world—its behavioural aspect—was seemingly collapsed into rules. Conceivably, a theory of law might surmount this problem, first, by examining legal relationality—which I will do in chapter 7—and, secondly, by theorising within a Weberian *social action* frame of reference that gives appropriate weight to normativity:

[1] Talcott Parsons, *The Structure of Social Action*, (The Free Press, Glencoe, 2nd ed. 1949), 76–7.

the normative dimension of the legal world. From this (latter) standpoint, a legal system would be looked upon not merely as a system of legal rules, but as a symbiotic arrangement of, first, legal rules (and related concepts) and, secondly, organised institutional social structures. The aim of this approach is to restore the human individual as social actor to a central place within the theoretical enterprise and to escape from the distorting notion of the law as a machine running by itself. A decisive shift of emphasis from the legal rule as an object of theoretical enquiry to human action—of which rules are seen as merely a component—would mark a significant repositioning of some central theoretical concerns of Hartian jurisprudence—particularly Hart's emphasis upon legal rules—within a classical sociology context. It is clear that in *The Concept of Law*,[2] Hart sets himself the task of examining, among other things, the legal rule without being necessarily oblivious to the wider action frame of reference within which legal rules may be situated. Classical sociology in its Weberian variant, taking action as the relevant frame of reference, located norms and their functioning *within* that broader context. In Weberian sociology there was a place for analysing norms as a component of human action. In Hart's theory there was no specific place for analysing action *per se*: an action frame of reference was, at best, merely implicit and largely unarticulated. Yet an analysis of Hartian "*social* rules" that did not at least presuppose the human behavioural context in which those rules play a role would have been scarcely intelligible.

Normativity in action

The centrality of the normative component of human action was emphasised by the American sociologist Talcott Parsons (1902–1979), one of the principal mid-twentieth century American exponents of Max Weber's sociology. In contrast to Weber, Parsons virtually *equated* human action with effort to conform with norms. This is clear from the passage quoted at the beginning of this chapter. While at various points Weber

[2] H L A Hart, *The Concept of Law* (Clarendon Press, Oxford, 2nd ed. 1994) (*CL*).

stressed the importance of the normative component of human action, he did not actually define action *as* normatively oriented behaviour. At one point, for instance, Weber describes a type of social action which—despite having all the characteristics of normatively oriented action in terms of stability, invariance, uniformity and so on—is in fact almost entirely governed by the pursuit of individual ends: that is, it is instrumentally rational action, a type of *zweckrational* action, to use Weber's terminology.[3] Parsons perhaps overstated his position in seemingly asserting that action—that is, (all) human behaviour—has a normative component. Certainly most instances of behaviour that can be regarded as "stable" or uniformly patterned may have a normative dimension. Without diminishing the significance to Parsons of the normative component of human action, it is possible to discern a more moderate version of Parsons' theoretical stance where stability and patterning of human action are present, yet "action" is not actually *defined as* "effort to conform with norms".

Parsons' linkage of social interaction and norms is an appropriate point of introduction for an examination, in this chapter, of the normative dimension of human social action. If the social system can be regarded as a system of action at least partly made up of normatively oriented interactions of individuals, in what sense and to what extent—it may be asked—do *legal* norms feature as a component of "social systems"? In other words, what role, if any, do legal norms play in structuring processes of social action or interaction? These are the main questions to be examined in this chapter. In considering them, I will seek to demonstrate how Weber's action frame of reference might provide a basis for approaching a resolution of the problems underlying the Second Gordian Knot. Our point of departure, then, is Weber's concept of social action and related concepts of social interaction and social relationship.

---

[3] Max Weber, *The Theory of Social and Economic Organization* (The Free Press, New York, 1947) (*TSEO*), 122. Weber gives as an example the dealers in a market who treat their own actions as a means for obtaining the satisfaction of the ends defined by what they realise to be their own typical economic interests (see *TSEO*, 112).

Social Action, Interaction and Hart's Concept of "Social Rule"

In sociology, interaction has been analysed as a "process" taking place "between two or more actors". According to Parsons and Shils, the interaction of ego and alter is the most elementary form of social system.[4] One person cannot, in any meaningful social sense, "interact" with himself or herself. Interaction may be seen as mutual social action (in Weber's sense of action "oriented to the past, present or expected future behaviour of others") in which each participant acts, or orients his or her action, with respect to the other participant(s).[5] Parsons' concept of interaction closely resembles Weber's concept of the *social relationship*. Weber defines "social relationship" as "the behaviour of a plurality of actors in so far as, in its meaningful content, the action of each takes account of that of the others and is oriented in these terms".[6] Weber adds that as a defining criterion, "it is essential that there should be at least a minimum of mutual orientation of the action of each to that of the others".[7] The meaningful content of a social relationship—its subjective meaning—can be various. Weber's examples include conflict, hostility, sexual attraction, friendship, loyalty or economic exchange. *Norms* or "maxims", according to Weber, govern the constant or stable components of a social relationship:[8]

> "The meaningful content which remains relatively constant in a social relationship is capable of formulation in terms of maxims which the parties concerned expect to be adhered to by their partners, on the average and approximately."

Parsons similarly comments that "within the action frame of reference, stable interaction implies that acts acquire 'meanings' which are interpreted with reference to a common set of nor-

[4] Talcott Parsons, Edward A Shils *et al.* (eds.), *Toward a General Theory of Action* (Harvard University Press, Cambridge, Mass., 1951), 55 and 105.

[5] *TSEO*, 112. For Weber, "action is social in so far as, by virtue of the subjective meaning attached to it by the acting individual (or individuals), it takes account of the behaviour of others and is thereby oriented in its course" (*TSEO*, 88).

[6] Ibid., 118.

[7] Ibid.

[8] Ibid., 120.

mative conceptions".[9] Action is at least partly explicable through an identification of the norms that individuals use, on the one hand, to evaluate and to "orient" or modify their own social action and, on the other hand, to evaluate and act upon the action, social or otherwise, of others.

In his discussion of chess as a stable "system of interaction", Parsons gives prominence to the normative dimension of human interaction. Parsons acknowledges some of the ways in which social norms (e.g., the rules of a game) feature as a component of meaningful social action, identifying at least four levels of "meaning". First, players are motivated to participate. This may be seen to correspond to Weber's *wertrational* (value rational) mode of orientation of action. An individual may act in accordance with the value that participation in the game for its own sake is a "good thing". Players may treat this value as a sufficient ground for participating, without further justification. Secondly, the pursuit of a goal, such as the desire to win, has a clear association with Weber's *zweckrational* (purpose rational) mode of orientation of action. The desired end is winning the game or, possibly, the will to achieve a kind of intellectual domination of an opponent: perhaps especially so in the case of chess. Thirdly, strategies for play may involve rational formulation of particular means of gaining advantages which, taken cumulatively, enable the more skilful player to win the game. Fourthly, stability of the conduct of the game—a stabilised system of interaction—is achieved by players adhering to—in other words, orienting their action by reference to—the rules of the game. Adherence to the mutually accepted rules of the game stabilises the expectations of each player with respect to the action of the other player and enables interaction to proceed continuously on the same basis. Now, whilst "meaning" is conceivable on many different levels, the normative component of interaction is a critical element since it has a bearing on meaning at every level: motivation to participate, pursuit of goals, formulation of strategies, and stability of conduct of the game.[10]

[9] Talcott Parsons, "An Outline of the Social System", in Talcott Parsons, Edward Shils *et al.* (eds.) *Theories of Society* (The Free Press of Glencoe Inc., 1961), Vol. I, 41.

[10] Ibid.

Like Parsons, Hart occasionally used chess and other games as a means of explaining the normative component of social behaviour. In *The Concept of Law*, Hart refers to the rules of chess (among other types of rules) as "social rules", loosely basing his concept of "social rule" around that of a "social group" and its behavioural patterns. Whereas Parsons uses chess as a model to illustrate essential components of human interaction and to highlight aspects of the functioning of social norms in the context of social interaction, Hart uses chess to illustrate the internal aspect of "social rules".[11] Chess players, according to Hart, have a reflective critical attitude to the patterns of behaviour involved in playing chess, e.g., moving the queen in a certain way. Each player moves the queen and other playing pieces in a manner prescribed by the rules and demands conformity to the rules when deviation is actual or threatened. Critical normative language may be used when a player contravenes the rules. Hart gives a few examples: " 'I (You) ought not to have moved the Queen like that', 'I (You) must do that', 'That is right', 'That is wrong' ".[12] Although the features of his notion of "social group" are not explored in detail, Hart's discussion of the relationship between "social rules" and "social group" appears—at least on the basis of his use of the chess game model—to be predicated on an interactional conception of social group, echoing mainstream sociological analysis.[13] Hart links "social rules" to behavioural patterns of group interaction in holding that a "social rule" exists if some members of a social group look upon a course of behaviour as a general standard to be followed by the group as a whole. In a similar context Weber's understanding of "existence" (of social norms) is linked to the notion of "empirical validity". For sociological purposes the validity of a norm is judged according to the extent to which it functions as

---

[11] *CL*, 56–7.

[12] *CL*, 57.

[13] See A M Honoré, "Groups, Laws, and Obedience", in A W B Simpson (ed.), *Oxford Essays in Jurisprudence* (Clarendon Press, Oxford, 1973), ch. 1; also A M Honoré, "What is a Group?" (1975) 61 *Archiv für Rechts-und-Sozialphilosophie*, 161 *et seq.*

an actual determinant of human conduct.[14] If an actor, by virtue of the subjective meaning of action, orients his or her conduct by reference to a social norm and does so to an empirically measurable degree—for example, in terms of a statable probability—then the norm, for Weber, is empirically valid. It has actually determined human conduct.

As we have seen, a "social rule", according to Hart, engenders externally observable regularities of behaviour, whilst "internally"—that is, in terms of its "internal aspect"—the relevant standard is characterised by a "critical reflective attitude" towards certain behaviour. This attitude involves a measure of "acceptance" of the relevant standard and, following Neil MacCormick's discussion, at least two further elements:[15]

1. a cognitive (evaluative) element: where group members engage in the activity of conceiving of certain behaviour as conforming, not conforming or being irrelevant to a given standard; and
2. a volitional (critical) element: where group members engage in the activity of "desiring" or "preferring" that certain behaviour should conform to a given standard.

How, and where, is the relevant standard defined? In the legal context, definitive formulations of particular rules are usually to be found in an "authoritative" source such as (say) a statute. For example, there can surely be no more definitive formulation of the rule in a specific section of a statute than the *actual words* used in the section. But there are practical difficulties where rules, which Hart describes as "social rules", have *no* definitive expression in a source regarded as "authoritative". How is the content of such a rule to be expressed? That you ought to have acted in manner φ under circumstances N may be more than an *ex post facto* expression of criticism or disapproval in response to your failure so to act. It contains a formulation of the standard

[14] See Max Weber, *Economy and Society. An Outline of Interpretive Sociology* (Bedminster Press Inc., New York, 1968) (*ES*), 312; and Max Weber, *Max Weber on Law in Economy and Society* (Harvard University Press, Cambridge, Mass., 1954) (*LES*), 12.

[15] Neil MacCormick, *H.L.A. Hart* (Edward Arnold (Publishers) Ltd., London, 1981), 33–4.

that you, if not a class of persons that includes you, ought to act in manner φ under circumstances N, regardless of the origin of, or basis for, this standard. If "criticism" includes, in some form, a statement of the "social rule" embodying the relevant standard of behaviour, that statement may be as definitive a formulation as it is possible to find, provided there exists no competing formulation regarded, in some sense, as "authoritative". It may be, then, that factors which Hart presents as mere external *manifestations* of the critical reflective attitude (particularly "criticism" expressed in normative language such as "ought", "right" and "wrong") are in some sense actually *constitutive* of the applicable standard.

In the *Postscript* to *The Concept of Law*, Hart refers to "social rules" as "custom-type rules of any social group large or small".[16] Hart comments that his original analysis of "social rules" applied only to certain limited situations, including "ordinary social customs (which may or may not be recognized as having legal force)" and certain important legal rules, including the rule of recognition. He points out that his analysis of "social rules" did not apply to *enacted* legal rules which "exist as legal rules from the moment of their enactment".[17] In that context, Hart is perhaps (rightly) distinguishing between the *existence conditions* of, on the one hand, "social rules" in the sense of custom-type rules whose existence is constituted, as Hart puts it, "by a form of social practice" and, on the other hand, enacted legal rules whose existence is dependent on satisfaction of validity criteria, and presumably enactment conditions, specified in a rule of recognition. But, as Hart apparently concedes in the *Postscript*, his analysis of "social rules" surely had wider import in terms of being applicable to legal rules of *both* the customary and enacted variety. For Hart makes the point that his analysis was originally conceived to "draw attention to the distinction between internal and external statements of law and between internal and external aspects of law". Hart had sought to explain those distinctions "by examining not the highly complex case of a legal system which comprises both enacted and custom-type

[16] *CL*, 255.
[17] Ibid., 256.

rules, but the simpler case (*to which the same distinctions between internal and external apply*) of the custom-type rules of any social group . . .".[18] It is arguable that Hart's analysis of "social rules" is—and *was*, in *The Concept of Law* as originally published—part of a more ambitious strategy to begin to explain behavioural modes generally associated with rule-governed behaviour: for example, the consensual, cognitive and volitional behavioural modes identified, by way of analytical elaboration of Hart's stance, by MacCormick. Those modes of behaviour can be viewed in sociological terms as aspects of meaningfully norm-oriented social action. It would follow that the resultant Hartian analysis of "social rules" is valid irrespective of the particular type of rule under investigation to the extent that such type of rule can possess an "internal aspect" and an "external aspect" in the sense that Hart envisages. Depending on the context, and despite Hart's revised (*Postscript*) position, customary *and enacted* legal rules could thus be said to possess these "aspects".

But, in any event, in the final analysis Hart's clarifying account of the concept of "social rule" in the *Postscript*—responding to a number of criticisms made by Dworkin—although illuminating, ventures scarcely further into the realm of sociology and its concepts such as action and interaction. Hart does not use the *Postscript*—just as he did not, in any significant way, use *The Concept of Law* as originally published—for a sustained exploration of analytical issues surrounding the relationship between "social rules" and social behaviour. The importance of those issues in the present context, however, necessitates further discussion. Hart's omission, in other words, provides an opportunity to press the enquiry further. For it is already clear enough from the foregoing discussion that there are linkages between, on one hand, a Weberian concept of social action and its variants—i.e., social interaction, social relationship—and, on the other hand, a concept of the social norm based around a particular interpretation of Hart's concept of "social rule", but with a wider analytical reach. I have noted a marked commonality in the substance of Hart's and Parsons'

---

[18] *CL*, 254–5 (emphasis added).

respective discussions of chess as, in effect, a system of interaction dependent upon norms (or, in the case of Hart's analysis, "social rules") as structural points of reference. Further, whilst Hart does not use the terms "social", "social group", "social rule" or similar expressions in any technical sociological or legal sense, there is nothing in principle to suggest any broad inconsistency between his usage and usage of similar terminology in the work of Weber and Parsons. It seems appropriate then to examine in closer detail the linkages between Weber's concept of social action and the concept of the social norm on the basis:

1. that the structural features of a concept of social action may assist us to understand structural features and some of the basic functions of the social norm; and, conversely
2. that structural features of a concept of social norm and its basic functions may assist us to understand the structure of social action.

The hypothesis pursued here is this. If certain types of *legal* norms can be regarded as social norms in the sense of the discussion to follow, any points of interface between the social world and the legal world highlighted in the discussion may serve as a further step towards addressing the question posed at the commencement of this chapter: In what sense and to what extent do *legal* norms feature as a component of "social systems"?

Structural Features of Social Action and Social Norms

As a starting point, Weber's concept of social action—a "social system" according to Parsons' terminology—is "normatively neutral" in the sense that the presence of norms is not a necessary, or defining, characteristic. Action is "social" if it is modified (or "oriented") in response to one or more *others* or to the past, present or anticipated future behaviour of one or more *others*. Clearly, it makes no sense to speak of the realm of the "social" unless at least *two* human beings are involved. The smallest possible interactional grouping involves two individuals. Both Hart and Parsons in different ways base distinct analyses on this, the most elementary, form of social system: the interaction of ego and alter, exemplified by a game such as chess. At its most basic and abstract level that is the structure of social action as perceived by Weberian sociology.

Against that background, what is it that makes a *norm*—a human behavioural norm—"social"? What, in other words, are the distinguishing features of a *social* norm? If social action is a process involving the relationship between at least two interacting individuals, in what sense does a norm governing human behaviour reflect this dynamic? It is suggested that these questions may be approached under three broad headings: (i) the structural elements of norms; (ii) the concept of relationality; and (iii) the concept of functionality.

To begin with, what structural elements of norms can be identified? Let us assume a simple concept of a human behavioural norm in the sense of a standard—embodying the notion of "ought"—whereby specified behaviour is rendered in some sense obligatory or non-optional. The norm requires an act to be performed or desisted from: e.g., "Max ought to (or shall) ϕ". Now let us further imagine background social conditions in which at least a minimal "system of interaction"—not less than two persons acting with respect to one another—is present. The same formulation—"Max ought to (or shall) ϕ"—when seen in that *social* setting has a particular signification. The relevant behaviour (ϕ-ing) is not non-optional, as it were, in a social vacuum. The interests and expectations of persons *other than* the obligated party are of consequence. Such an elementary social context renders a norm such as "Max ought to (or shall) ϕ" socially intelligible provided there is at least one person (other than Max) *relative to whom it is the case that Max ought to ϕ:* for example, Maxine. Max's ϕ-ing is then not merely ϕ-ing for its own sake. It is ϕ-ing in a social context: a context involving Max *and* Maxine. Maxine may *expect* Max to ϕ because, in applying the relevant norm to their situation, Max ought to ϕ relative to Maxine. At this point a rudimentary notion of social relationality—expressed in terms of *correlativity* and reflected in the structure of the operative behavioural norm—begins to emerge. In his analysis of legal concepts (or "conceptions") partially in terms of correlatives, W N Hohfeld drew attention to the relationality inhering in social behaviour and in the norms that govern it. Hohfeld, of course, was not a sociologist. As a jurist, the main focus of his attention was on legal concepts. But an examination of situations outside the legal setting demonstrates, *with the benefit of Hohfeld's insight*, the pervasive relationality underlying social behaviour which is reflected not only in the structure of the social norm, but in the structure of key *legal* concepts. It seems, on the face of it, a curious prospect to apply Hohfeldian insight towards the attainment of an improved understanding of the social world, whilst at the same time seeking to unravel aspects of the social dimension of the legal world. Yet in Hohfeld that prospect begins to be realised. A more detailed consideration of Hohfeldian relationality follows in chapter 7 below.

In order to pursue our enquiry initially in the non-institutional (non-legal) setting, it is useful again to focus attention on the game of chess. At the most general level we might say that the rules of chess are capable of being formulated in terms that *one player* ought to act in a certain manner (e.g., to perform certain "moves" of playing pieces) in accordance with the rules of chess and thus in fulfilment of the expectations of the *other player*. If we seek some justification of the rules themselves and their applicability in a specific context, we may find it in the fact that the players have agreed between themselves—or promised to one another—to abide by the rules. In itself that is a normative process because it may presuppose some moral precept that one ought to fulfil one's promises. That aspect however, though highly significant, is beyond the scope of the present discussion. It is sufficient for the moment to attend to the rules of chess in themselves and to regard those rules as constituting *reason enough* for players to act in a particular manner, i.e., in accordance with the rules.

On that basis, then, let us assume that the actions of the players in question—to be referred to as "ego" and "alter"—are governed by a norm that can initially be formulated as follows:

> Under circumstances N, alter shall act in manner φ relative to ego.

In chess, "circumstances N" might include the fact that ego and alter have resolved to play chess (at all), that it is alter's turn,

128

and that alter chooses to move a particular playing piece, for example the bishop: such a move being the substance of "act ϕ". Assuming that all relevant conditioning circumstances obtain, then, a more specific formulation of the norm might be:

> Under circumstances N, alter shall move the bishop playing piece diagonally (and otherwise in accordance with the rules of chess) relative to ego.

What is important here is that ego and alter stand in a particular relationship to one another. According to the norm, alter must perform the act ϕ, whilst ego need not actually "do" anything. That is not to say that ego has no role as such to play. Ego may, in fact, tacitly acknowledge the act of ϕ-ing, given that he is in a sense a "passive beneficiary" of the act. He will doubtless have "expectations" that alter will perform the act, and he may use persuasion or encouragement to induce her to ϕ if she is reluctant to do so. If the norm should happen to be a legal norm, ego might have to take positive action (e.g., through litigation) to compel performance from alter. But in the present context ego's role is seemingly "passive" or expectational, whilst alter's role is essentially "active" or performative.

In normatively guided human behaviour, especially normatively stabilised interaction, "expectations" have a key role, as Parsons points out:[19]

> "A stable system of interaction . . . orients its participants in terms of mutual expectations, which have the dual significance of expressing normative evaluations and stating contingent predictions of overt behavior. This mutuality of expectations implies that the *evaluative* meanings of acts are shared by the interacting units in two ways: what a member does can be categorized in terms meaningful to both; also, they share criteria of behavior, so that there are common standards of evaluation for particular acts."

The shared expectations and mutually acknowledged obligations of those participating in social interaction create a context in which participants come to rely on the probability of future conduct following the same pattern. This may result in stability,

[19] Parsons, above at n. 9, at 42.

implying, in turn, the possibility of repeatability. The existence of norms may thus heighten ego's expectation that alter will act in a particular manner. As Weber remarks:[20]

> "An important (but not indispensable) component of social action is its meaningful orientation to the *expectation* that *others* will act in a certain way, and to the presumable chances of success for one's *own* action resulting therefrom."

The presence of mutual "expectations" (each participant having an expectation of how the others should act) does not imply that a participant expects the others to act in the *same* way. In a given context the *norm* specifies the content of the act to be performed. This may or may not be an identical type of action for each participant. The norm itself functions as a determinant, or partial determinant, of the action expected of each participant.[21]

Taking the chess example to a further stage, we might introduce into the model the more specific—and, as it were, more distinctly "Hohfeldian"—language of "right" and "duty" without necessarily assuming a legal context or a context in which alter's situation is perceived in terms (say) of moral obligation. The reformulation of the norm in terms of the correlative notions of "right" and "duty" simply reflects more concretely the position of the parties *relative to one another.*

Under circumstances N:

(i) alter has a *duty* to ϕ relative to ego; and
(ii) ego has a *right* relative to alter that alter should ϕ.[22]

At this point we might note what is perhaps inordinately obvious: that the rules of chess govern how players move playing pieces and not how playing pieces themselves "move". It is certainly true to a degree that the rules "attach" in some way to the playing pieces, for example in the sense that the bishop may be thought of as a playing piece which may only move diagonally,

---

[20] *ES*, 1375 (Weber's emphasis and emphasis added).

[21] Weber links the idea of "expectation" to the concept of a (legal) "right": see *ES*, 327; and the discussion in ch. 7 below.

[22] The concept of Hohfeldian "jural correlatives" is discussed more fully in ch. 7 below.

and so on. Here we attribute the property of diagonal movement to the bishop rather than to a player. But the point to be emphasised is that the rules operate to regulate the relationship between players: that is, the action of players *with respect to one another*. Looked at this way, the rules define what players do, not what "bishops" (i.e., playing pieces) do.

In the chess example, then, alter has a duty to move the bishop playing piece diagonally (and otherwise in accordance with the rules of chess) relative to ego. Thus:

Under circumstances N:

(i) alter has a duty relative to ego to move the bishop playing piece diagonally (and otherwise in accordance with the rules of chess); and

(ii) ego has a right relative to alter that alter should move the bishop playing piece diagonally (and otherwise in accordance with the rules of chess).

This formulation of what is in fact a duty-imposing (or right′↔duty) social norm as opposed to a power-conferring (or power′↔liability) norm facilitates the identification of at least the following structural features:[23]

1. a description of "operative facts": the factual state of affairs that must obtain for the norm to become operative—in this case, circumstances N;

2. identification criteria of persons of inherence: i.e., those having an "expectation" or "right" that other persons should act in a prescribed manner—in this case, ego;

3. identification criteria of persons of incidence: i.e., those having a "duty" to act in a prescribed manner—in this case, alter;

4. deontic operator (e.g., "shall", "will", "may", "ought", "should", etc.);

5. description of an act, act-situation, action or course of action prescribed as being non-optional, i.e., the subject of the

---

[23] The structural features identified here are based on separate analyses of John Finnis and J W Harris. See John Finnis, *Natural Law and Natural Rights* (Clarendon Press, Oxford, 1980), 218–9; and J W Harris, *Law and Legal Science* (Clarendon Press, Oxford, 1979), 20–1 and 84. See also the discussion of Hohfeldian "operative facts" in chs. 5 and 7.

obligation or duty—in this case, the act φ (or otherwise the move of the bishop playing piece).

The most obvious context in which duty-imposing (or right↔duty) norms can be formulated in this way is, of course, the legal context, though it is clear that norms having an identical structure are to be found in non-institutional settings such as that of a game. A social norm may not contain all of these features together. Indeed, few *legal* norms are formulated in such specific terms. It takes little effort to imagine norms formulated in terms such as: "A has a duty to φ", or "A has a right to φ", or "A has a right to that book" or "one ought to φ". Norms so formulated conceal their *social* dimension because certain important matters are left unstated. For example, the formulation "A has a duty to φ" does not identify the person of inherence, who has a right that B should φ. Similarly, the formulation "A has a right to φ" does not reveal the identity of persons of incidence, who have duties to A.

Relationality: the Social Norm as a Linking Medium

The realm of the "social" is built into the very fabric of a norm that requires one individual to act in a certain manner *relative to one or more other individuals*. In relevant circumstances, such a norm may be regarded as being at least partly definitive of a social relationship, in Weber's sense, where the action of each of a plurality of actors, in its meaningful content, takes account of others or their action and is oriented in those terms. By having regard to a *norm* that requires alter to φ relative to ego, both ego and alter may be in some sense taking account of—and orienting their action by reference to—the past, present or anticipated behaviour and likely expectations of one another. The social norm describes what alter is required to do. Moreover, we can infer from the norm the presumed content of ego's expectation that what is required to be done by alter will in fact be done. An empirically and inter-subjectively valid social norm constitutes a *linking medium* or common point of reference between those whose action it governs. Action is *conceived* in relational terms by reference to the norm. The mere perception of certain actions may constitute part of what links actors ideatively. As each actor experiences the overt behaviour of every other actor this, in a minimal sense, links the participants in a shared experience of "external events". In cases where interaction is governed by social norms the connecting principles of identity, similarity or resemblance are present at a number of levels broadly corresponding to the structural features of the social norm identified above. In the chess example, for instance, these principles are present on at least the following levels. First, there is identity in that ego and alter recognise that the right and duty relate to the same subject matter: the act, to be performed by alter, of moving the bishop playing piece in conformity with the rules. Secondly, each actor recognises that the act in question is to be performed by the *same* person: alter. Thirdly, each actor knows the identity of his or her "opposite number": e.g., ego knows that both ego himself and alter are involved in the interaction. Fourthly, each actor knows that the same norm governs their conduct, and there is identity to a greater or lesser extent in the mind of each actor as to the evaluative and orientative meanings of actions. (This aspect is discussed in greater detail below under functionality.)

Revisiting the question of what it is that makes a norm governing human behaviour a "social" norm, it can be seen that a norm of the duty-imposing (or right↔duty) type may be described as "social" to the extent that it requires at least one party in specified circumstances to engage in a course of social action aimed at satisfying the expectations of at least one other party.[24] The "other" party's expectations may (or may not) be justified by the basis upon which the norm is imposed or is otherwise applicable to the conduct in question. A social norm may be justified, for instance, on moral or other grounds. Clearly, there may be other factors justifying the presence or existence of "social rules", which (rules), in turn, justify the action governed by the rules. However, those issues—important and interesting as they are—lie beyond the immediate scope of the present discussion.

---

[24] Power-conferring (or power↔liability) norms—which it is beyond the scope of this book to consider—operate differently and in a more complex way, but ultimately to no less effect as "social" norms.

The essentially social dynamic underlying behaviour governed by social norms, therefore, is demonstrated with some degree of clarity in the structural features of duty-imposing (or right′↔duty) social norms and in the relationality engendered by norms governing social action where the norms constitute a linking medium between social actors. The same social dynamic is demonstrated in a different way when considering how, in a practical sense, social norms are actually *used* by individuals in the context of social interaction. In other words, by considering the practical matter of *functionality*, it is possible to perceive, from a slightly different perspective, the social underpinnings of normatively guided human behaviour.

Functionality: Basic Functions of Social Norms

I propose to consider three basic functions of social norms that accentuate the social dynamic underlying behaviour governed by such norms. These are:

(A) the evaluative function
(B) the orientative function
(C) the regulatory function

(A) the evaluative function

The evaluative function of social norms broadly corresponds to the "cognitive" element of Hart's concept of "social rule" highlighted by MacCormick.[25] Group members conceive of certain behaviour as conforming, not conforming or being irrelevant to a given standard embodied in a "social rule". Clearly, a social norm may be used as a standard against which to evaluate or judge human behaviour. As we have seen, Weber held that action is "social" in so far as by virtue of the subjective meaning attached to it by an actor (e.g., ego), it takes account of the behaviour of others (e.g., alter), and is thereby oriented in its course. In taking account of alter's behaviour or anticipated behaviour ego may ascribe evaluative meaning by virtue of a social norm either:

---

[25] MacCormick, above at n. 15, at 33–4.

(i) to his *own* behaviour, e.g., anticipating a possible adverse or "critical" response from alter if he (ego) should fail to comply with a duty imposed by the relevant norm; or

(ii) to *alter's* behaviour, e.g., evaluating alter's behaviour in terms of whether it complies with a duty imposed by the relevant norm.

A key function of the social norm, then, is as a reference point for the evaluation by an individual of *that individual's own* social action. A further important function is as a reference point for the evaluation by one individual (ego) of the behaviour of *another* individual (alter). In the course of playing chess, for example, players continuously evaluate their *own* behaviour (consciously or unconsciously) and that of the other player in terms of whether it conforms to the rules: for example, ensuring that the bishop playing piece is moved only diagonally rather than laterally, and so on. In each case, the act of evaluation involves the actor in a purely mental judgmental act about the applicability or non-applicability (and the manner, incidence, method or appropriateness of applicability or non-applicability) of a social norm with respect to behaviour in a given case. As we have seen, an act of evaluation may involve a judgment that a given course of action, whether past, present or anticipated, complies with the prescription contained in a relevant norm. The evaluation in question may comprise ego's judgment relative to his own past, present or intended future action, or ego's judgment relative to alter's past, present or anticipated future action. Evaluative judgments may be of various kinds and are not limited to whether an act *complies* with a norm. For example: is an act *intra vires* or *ultra vires* in relation to a power? Is a legal instrument valid or invalid relative to conditions for its constitution? Does someone have "capacity" to act in a certain way? Is an argument within or beyond the scope of a doctrine?

(B) the orientative function

Another basic function of a social norm is as a reference point for the orientation by an individual of *that individual's* social action. In *The Concept of Law*, Hart refers to rules as "guides" for conduct. Weber, as we have seen, refers to norms as "causes" or "determinants" of human action.[26] The orientative function of social norms in the present context is understood basically in the sense of guides, causes or determinants of action.

Whereas an act of evaluation may be a purely mental judgmental act, an act of "orientation", by contrast, can be seen to involve:

(i) a "mental" aspect being the purposive mental effort to modify one's action in a certain way, *following upon an act of evaluation* in the sense described; and

(ii) an overt or "externally" perceptible action which is the realisation (whether successful or unsuccessful) of the mental effort. The overt action might consist of muscular movement of some sort.

Orientation of action by reference to a social norm may be seen as the *outcome* of a process that involves an act of evaluation. The use of a social norm for the evaluation by ego of alter's behaviour is part of the ostensible function of the social norm as a reference point for the orientation of *ego's* social action. What ego does depends on his perception of whether alter has acted, or failed to act, in compliance with an appropriate norm. Ego's act of "orientation" follows upon an act of "evaluation" of alter's behaviour by reference to the norm. If, alternatively, the evaluative act relates to *ego's* intended action he would use the social norm to evaluate in advance his intended action in terms of whether it complies with the norm.

The expression "orientation" conveys the idea of a conscious modification of behaviour consisting of an effort of will to produce external acts which induce a perceptible change in the "real world". The purely mental act of evaluation may be of sociological interest only where it leads to orientation of action, even if that is merely a manifestation of the content of the evaluative act, for example a verbal acknowledgement that a certain act complies with a social norm, or criticism for a perceived failure to comply with a norm. When it is said that a social norm func-

---

[26] *ES*, 312; *LES*, 12. Hart also speaks of rules as a guide to, and *justification* for, action: see, e.g., *CL*, 11, 89 and 90. See Joseph Raz, *The Concept of a Legal System* (Clarendon Press, Oxford, 1980), 156 *et seq.*

tions "as a reference point", the suggestion is that the norm is referred to as an idea: a motivating normative idea embodying the notion of "ought" (or "shall" or "must") in relation to human behaviour. A norm does not in any sense physically enact human behaviour. It is an ought-proposition which may constitute a reason or motivation for action. The expression "reference point" thus denotes that a norm is a proposition *referred to* for the purpose of evaluating and orienting human action. A social norm may, of course, be only one of a complex of motivating ideas constituting the subjective meaning of a course of action.

Orientation of action by reference to a social norm may be compliant or non-compliant orientation. The norm may constitute a reason for acting in some way *other than* that prescribed: civil disobedience being one example.

(C) the regulatory function

From the discussion we can assert a further basic function of the social norm which is as a means of *regulating* the action of one or more individuals relative to one or more other individuals. This function is based on the recognition that individuals, in evaluating and orienting their social action by reference to social norms, take account of the behaviour of "others" in the sense either that they expect "others" to act in the manner prescribed by a given norm or that they feel obligated to act in that manner in fulfilment of the expectation of "others".

The regulatory function is also based on the recognition that when action is so oriented, it is social action at least in the sense that it involves the individual in taking account of the behaviour of others by acknowledging the normativity of the social environment which consists of innumerable "others" who both promulgate, and also evaluate and orient their social action by reference to, social norms. More concretely, a social norm is intelligible in a social context in which "egos", in acting socially, take account of "alters" or the behaviour of "alters". A social norm reflects this relationality by embodying an "oughtness" with respect either to (i) the action of ego (where ego's behaviour is governed by a norm) or (ii) the action of alter (where alter's behaviour is so

137

governed) assuming a context in which ego is acting socially relative to alter.

Social norms may furthermore be used as a means of inducing individuals to act in a certain way and may often be used in combination with other types of inducement, e.g., physical or psychological coercion.

Social action and legal norms

The overarching question pursued in this chapter is this: In what sense, and to what extent, do *legal* norms feature as a component of "social systems"? In other words, what role, if any, do legal norms play in structuring processes of social action or interaction? If certain legal norms can be regarded as social norms in the sense suggested above, it follows that the relationship between social norms and social action, as discussed, will broadly hold for legal norms. Legal norms of the duty-imposing (or right↔duty) type *do*, by and large, fit the analysis of social norms discussed in this chapter. Many points of interface between the social world and (so far as separable) the legal world may thus be inferred from that discussion. There are, however, aspects of the legal world—in particular, its *institutionality*—that make it unique. And whilst, as I aim to show, the institutionality of law in a number of key respects marks it apart from the remainder of the social world, legal norms—at the level of their use, application and function—correspondingly possess unique characteristics not possessed by non-legal social norms. Some of the more important points of uniqueness are considered in more detail in the following discussion.

Social Action and Legal Norms—Institutionality

As I have argued, a duty-imposing (or right↔duty) legal norm may be described as a "social norm" to the extent that it requires at least one party in specified circumstances to engage in a course of social action aimed at satisfying the expectations of at least one other party.[27] In many instances, legal norms fitting

[27] The expression "social action" is used broadly in Weber's sense: see, generally, ch. 2.

this broad concept of social norm will actually constitute an integral part of the meaningful content of social action or interaction *if* individuals use the norm as a reference point for the orientation of their action. For example, if alter has a legal (contractual) duty to pay £100 to ego, the legal norm (or derivative contractual norm) requiring payment of £100 may be empirically valid as between ego and alter in the Weberian sense that it functions *for them* as an actual determinant of their conduct. It is doubtless safe to say that legal systems generally owe their existence to the fact that, for much of the time, private citizens—as part of the meaningful component of their social action—consciously and knowingly orient their action by reference to relevant, applicable legal norms.[28]

But significantly, much legally relevant human behaviour—particularly at the level of the private citizen as opposed to the public official—is by no means social action in the sense of Weber's concept. In other words, it does not necessarily involve conscious orientation of behaviour in *any* sense, still less by reference to legal norms. For instance, the English law of negligence is largely based on the premise of unintentional action or inaction causing harm to others. Even where such action is

---

[28] In *The Concept of Law*, Hart acknowledges that one of the minimum conditions for the existence of a legal system is that legal rules, at the level of their practical application and use by private citizens, exhibit features that are integral to his concept of "social rule". He thus implies conscious orientation of behaviour by reference to legal rules. As we have seen, these features (following MacCormick) include consensual, cognitive and volitional elements where group members: (i) manifest "acceptance" of relevant standards or norms characterised by a "critical reflective attitude" towards certain behaviour; (ii) knowingly conceive of behaviour in terms of its conformity, disconformity or irrelevance to certain standards; and (iii) knowingly engage in the activity of "desiring" certain behaviour to conform to such standards. Hart comments that *legal* rules may be "accepted" as common standards of behaviour by private citizens who recognise an obligation to obey them. Citing the first of his two necessary and sufficient conditions for the existence of a legal system, Hart observes that "those rules of behaviour which are valid according to the system's ultimate criteria of validity must be generally obeyed . . . The first condition is the only one which private citizens *need* satisfy: they may obey each 'for his part only' and from any motive whatever; though in a healthy society they will in fact often accept these rules as common standards of behaviour and acknowledge an obligation to obey them, or even trace this obligation to a more general obligation to respect the constitution" (*CL*, 116–7 (Hart's emphasis)).

intentional, the particular consequences of the action may be unintended or unforeseen. The law may impose duties of care and standards of reasonable foreseeability which are quite remote from any thought that might have passed through an actor's mind in acting or failing to act. In other contexts the law may *assume* a particular state of affairs—which may or may not be, though is ultimately capable of imputation to, human behaviour—against the true state of affairs actually existing. This is the case with legal fictions. Legal fictions consist of a deliberate false assumption of facts against the true facts.

Often, the individual simply does not possess the mental disposition of "compulsion" or of "expectation" corresponding respectively to the presence of a legal duty imposed upon him or her or of a legal right with which he or she is invested. How can it be that infants, unborn children and mentally disabled persons possess legal rights irrespective of their particular state of knowledge and regardless of their powers of reason? The law abounds with situations where, irrespective of the mental disposition or particular state of knowledge of an acting individual, legal duties are imposed on that person or the person is invested with legal rights. The maxim of the law *ignorantia juris neminem excusat* illustrates the point that even if someone proceeds in blissful ignorance of the requirements of the criminal law, those requirements will be applicable nonetheless. Neil MacCormick points to a similarly engaging aspect of the legal world in an example drawn from the law of contract. MacCormick writes that passengers boarding a bus may be entirely unaware of the fact that they have entered into a contract, and emphasises that "the knowledge or opinion of particular passengers and drivers is totally immaterial to the proposition that there exist as many contracts as passengers".[29]

Superficially, none of this suggests anything more than the simple truth that the domain of law is the entire spectrum of human behaviour extending even to natural and fictional events, not merely social action, nor—narrower still—social action consciously oriented by reference to legal rules. But a more arcane

---

[29] Neil MacCormick, "Law as Institutional Fact" (1974) 90 *Law Quarterly Review*, 102 at 104.

truth is suggested by the fact that whether or not a private citizen is aware of, understands, or chooses to act upon his or her legal rights, duties, powers or liabilities, is in most cases immaterial to the proposition that those rights, duties, powers and liabilities exist in law and are capable for the most part of being given legal force and effect. What is suggested more specifically is that the legal world possesses a unique property based around two interrelated characteristics alluded to by MacCormick: (i) the distinctive *institutional perspective* from which legally relevant behaviour and other factual events are perceived, and (ii) the *institutionally ascriptive* nature of legal phenomena.

Thus, on one hand, MacCormick highlights an issue that is more fundamental than the mere assertion that the "typical" actor's interpretation of contract-instituting events may not coincide with a "legal interpretation" of the same events. An actor may engage in a course of social action which is subjectively meaningful by reference to relevant criteria of meaning applied by him or her to the action. In some cases, the actor's criteria of meaning may include a particular interpretation of legal norms. It is possible, however, that from a certain perspective—specifically an *institutional* point of view—the behaviour in question bears a meaning by reference to legal norms and other relevant institutional criteria of meaning which is entirely different from, though it *may* partially coincide with, that underlying the actor's behaviour. Indeed, often an actor may be entirely oblivious of other possible criteria of meaning by which relevant behaviour may be evaluated. On the other hand, a contract-instituting act or event such as that exemplified by MacCormick's omnibus scenario is significant to lawyers, though doubtless also to sociologists of law, because, as MacCormick later observes, "the law *ascribes* certain rights and duties to individuals conditionally upon the existence of contracts".[30] It need hardly be stated that the law does not merely ascribe *contractual* rights and duties: *all* legal rights, duties, powers and liabilities are in some sense ascribed by law.

In what sense do legal artefacts, such as right or duty, have an institutionally ascribed nature? What does it mean to suggest

[30] Ibid. (emphasis added).

that "the law ascribes" rights, duties, powers and liabilities? Just as for Kelsen "imputation" is an act of the intellect so "ascription" is a conceptual act. Yet it is *the law* that is said to "ascribe" rights, duties and such like. Does this suggest that it is possible to identify "the law" with a determinate human being such as an "Austinian" sovereign? In the context of the western form of bureaucratic state law, such an identification is surely a distortion of the idea of law. But we do customarily speak of legal phenomena as if the law were a person: "the law imposes liability", "the law confers a right", "the law allows an exemption", "the law creates an immunity", and so on. It would seem reasonable to account for this by acknowledging that, according to some accounts, the law is a uniquely human phenomenon created and organised by human beings for human beings. It is thus not surprising that law occasionally tends to be looked upon in anthropomorphic terms. But these linguistic usages in fact allude to the sense in which law possesses an institutionally ascriptive nature. In his essay, "Language and the Law", Glanville Williams—discussing the concept of a legal right—questions Vinogradoff's assumption that a legal right is a kind of claim:[31]

> "Now a claim is a psychological fact, a state of mind; but legal rights can "exist" in people who do not know of their existence, and so have not the mental attitude of claim. . . . Rights and duties are mental states, but they are not states of mind of the subjects of the rights and duties; they are states of mind of the persons asserting the legal rules."

Without doubt, rights and duties can be regarded as "states of mind" of persons asserting legal rules or applying the rules to situations of fact. They involve subjectively meaningful "states of mind", such as the conceptual act of perceiving the legal position of persons of inherence and of incidence in specifically relational terms. But Williams possibly overlooks the fact that the *subject* of a legal right or a duty may be, at one and the same time, the person who asserts or applies relevant legal rules. It is always possible for a subject to misperceive his or her legal posi-

---

[31] Glanville Williams, "Language and the Law" (Part V) (1946) 62 *Law Quarterly Review*, 387 at 398–9.

tion, of course; nor is such perception, in any event, an institutionally authoritative interpretation. Even where the subject is as well informed as it is possible to be, his or her interpretation may remain at variance with an "institutionally correct" interpretation of the legal state of affairs. An example is where two commercial organisations, benefiting from the expertise of the best available legal advice, enter into a carefully drafted agreement. In the context of a litigated dispute some time later they may find that the agreement has an entirely different legal effect from that intended. But that in itself takes us no closer to understanding the institutionally ascriptive nature of law. What Glanville Williams fails to point out is that it can matter what the office, status or identity is of the person who does the asserting or the ascribing. In other words it may be legally and sociologically more significant—depending on the investigator's particular interests—that one person (for instance, a judge in a court of law) rather than another person (for instance, a private individual on a bus) asserts the existence of a legal right or duty. As MacCormick notes, it matters that the law ascribes rights and duties because, in turn, what makes that matter:[32]

". . . is that sometimes people wish to assert legal rights and enforce legal duties, the procedures for doing which are established by further legal rules. And all that depends on the existence of organised groups of people, the legal profession, the courts, and enforcement officials, whose function is to give effect to such rules and whose actual practice is tolerably consonant with the announced rules."

The essentials of the ascriptive component of the adjudicatory function may be understood more clearly if we revisit the chess model discussed above and apply that model as the basis for a highly simplified image of a key aspect of the adjudicatory function.

We may first assume that an umpire has been introduced into the chess model. What function does the umpire perform in such a context? Briefly, the umpire does not "do" what the players "do", i.e., play the game. But, depending on the nature of the relationship between umpire and players, what the players

[32] MacCormick, above at n. 29, at 104.

do will be affected by what the umpire does if called upon to make a ruling, while, conversely, what the umpire does will be affected by what the players do. The umpire basically has a twofold function: that of making binding rulings as regards (i) the meaning of the action of the players by reference to the rules of the game, and (ii) the meaning of the rules of the game—the interpretation of the rules—in their *application* to the action of the players. An umpire may intervene in the event of a dispute between players as to either or both of matters (i) and (ii). In the legal context, a judge—for example, *Iudex*—would perform a broadly similar, though by no means identical, role. *Iudex* may be regarded as the embodiment of a legal institutional perspective.

If we substitute for chess players the parties to a litigated (e.g., civil law) dispute, there is the skeleton of a rudimentary model of adjudication. In that model the social action of *Iudex* and its attendant complexes of subjective meaning—not that of litigants—is an object of attention. Thus, *Iudex* meaningfully orients his or her official action by reference to legal norms. As part of that process, *Iudex* also ascribes evaluative meaning (by reference to similar criteria of meaning) to the behaviour of litigants (or to other "facts"). The Polish jurist Leon Petrażycki viewed ascription in terms of the metaphor of "projection". In his Introduction to Petrażycki's work *Law and Morality*, Nicholas Timasheff remarks that, according to Petrażycki, "the mental phenomena which form the reality of law, such as states of human minds ascribing rights and duties, possess the property of being *projected onto* the persons and things they concern".[33] Using Petrażycki's terminology, in the legal setting a meaning is "projected onto" the behaviour of others. The assumption at work here is this: that actor A's social action (e.g., that of *Iudex*) may be understandable only to an observer (e.g., a jurist) who is aware of the meaning which actor A ascribed to the behaviour of actor B (e.g., a litigant). If the task of sociology is to understand the social action of actor A (treated as

---

[33] Nicholas S Timasheff, Introduction to Leon Petrażycki, *Law and Morality* (Harvard University Press, Cambridge, Mass., 1955), xxvii–xxviii (emphasis added).

"ego"), and ego ascribes meaning to the behaviour of another actor (treated as "alter"), orienting his or her action accordingly, that ascription of meaning may be seen as part of the subjective meaning of ego's action. Thus, the official (social) action of *Iudex* (treated as "ego" for this purpose) is oriented at least partly by reference to the evaluative meaning which he or she ascribes to perceived states of "fact" (e.g., human behaviour) attributable to one or more others (treated as "alter"). Such meaning—authoritatively ascribed by reference to legal norms and other relevant criteria of meaning—constitutes the legal meaning of relevant "facts" or behaviour.

A substantive legal relationship—such as a Hohfeldian-type right↔duty jural relation (to be discussed further in chapter 7 below)—may be perceived as an ascription from the hypothetical viewpoint of *Iudex*. This image of the jural relation—that of a device which projects a conceptual linkage between polarised legal persons—can be visualised in the context of a simple diagram.

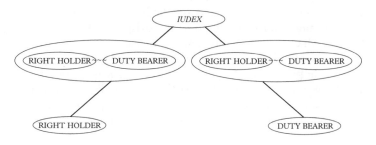

In the diagram the substantive legal relationship between right holder (RH) and duty bearer (DB) is perceived from the point of view of *Iudex*. *Iudex's* position *vis-à-vis* RH and DB respectively is partly defined by *Iudex's* perception of the substantive relationship. In other words, the adjective legal relationship between *Iudex* and each of RH and DB "contains" the substantive legal relationship obtaining between RH and DB—the RH–DB jural relation in the middle section of the diagram. Each "arm" of the diagram thus represents the respective poles of the individuated right↔duty jural relation. The left-hand side of the diagram represents *Iudex's* relationship to RH and incorporates *Iudex's* perception of RH's substantive right. The right-hand side of the diagram represents *Iudex's* relationship to DB and incorporates *Iudex's* perception of DB's substantive duty. Additionally, each term of the substantive legal relationship between RH and DB "contains" the notion of its correlative term.

The nature of law as an institutionally ascriptive phenomenon thus resides primarily in the official activities of organised institutional structures, specifically, the behaviour of public officials—judges—acting in an adjudicatory role. Those activities constitute social action in Weber's sense. The relationship between legal norms and *institutional* social action is of primary importance to the sociology of law. The social action or other behaviour of private citizens—and indeed other factual events—may be of immense sociological significance and interest. But such behaviour is not the key to understanding law's ascriptive nature. Where law assumes an institutional form in the sense of Weber's concept of "guaranteed law",[34] a "coercive apparatus" either possesses or responds to an adjudicatory function. Law in its institutional form presupposes the existence of legal institutions,[35] which include courts and tribunals, one of whose functions is to adjudicate upon the behaviour of litigants or others or to make appropriate rulings in relation to other relevant facts or events. We have seen that it is part of the adjudicatory function to confer evaluative meaning, in the sense of previous discussion, upon relevant factual states of affairs by reference to appli-

[34] *ES*, 313; *LES*, 13.

[35] See MacCormick, above at n. 29, at 110: "For there is another use of the term 'institution' which is also of great importance in relation to the law, but which is quite different from the well-established lawyer's notion of a 'legal institution' which I have just explicated. There are certain types of social system or sub-system, such as universities, schools, hospitals, orphanages, libraries, sporting organisations and the like, to which we often refer as 'institutions'. These are organisations of people which retain their organisational identity through time even though their personnel may change, because they are getting on with some job, and getting on with it in an organised way. Such I shall call 'social institutions'. To this class it is obvious that courts, parliaments, police forces, civil service departments, the Faculty of Advocates, and the Law Society, all belong". See also *ES*, 217 *et seq.* (legal authority with a bureaucratic administrative staff).

cable legal norms. On the basis of such ascriptions of evaluative meaning—legal meaning—relevant "coercive apparatuses" invested with significant social power are mobilised to take official enforcement action.

In the context of adjudication, the conferment of evaluative meaning involves a range of conceptual acts. One of these is the act of perceiving the legal position of legal persons (e.g., private individuals, litigants, corporate bodies) in relational terms: in other words, in terms of legal rights, duties, powers or liabilities. The "projection" of rights, duties and so on—the specific process of ascription—furthermore involves *authoritative* attributions of evaluative meaning, often regardless of the knowledge or understanding of the individuals most closely involved, e.g., that of a specific duty-bearer. In other words, under certain conditions the meaning ascribed by, and from the viewpoint of, public officials acting in a judicial role—as opposed to citizens in their private capacity—constitutes a legally conclusive ascription of meaning for the purposes of the legal system in question. In practice, conclusiveness is dependent upon all appellate procedures having been exhausted in a given case. But, more often than not, disputed issues are disposed of in inferior courts without the need to pursue an appeal to higher courts.

Developing legal relationality

In chapter 7 I will further develop the discussion of legal relationality by seeking a context in which legal relationships (Hohfeldian "jural relations") may be analysed as relationships of social power. I will focus in particular on the Hohfeldian right↔duty jural relation, as it is beyond the scope of this book to consider the Hohfeldian power↔liability jural relation in any detail. The implicit, unstated assumption underlying the discussion will be that legal relationships are theoretically conceived and ascribed (or projected) from the *Iudexian* point of view discussed in this and the preceding chapters. I will also consider some analytical aspects of Hohfeld's (and Hohfeldian) writings. One objective is to follow through the point made by Martin Krygier, following MacCormick, that sociology of law must begin with conceptual analysis and return to it continually. More specifically, chapter 7 takes as its point of departure Weber's observation that sociology looks to legal guarantees *and their underlying normative conceptions* as causes or consequences of perceived regularities. The legal relationship—perhaps more than any other "normative conception"—mirrors the inherent relationality of human social behaviour but in the context of its unique setting where, as I have argued, it may be perceived to have an "institutionally ascribed" character. W N Hohfeld recognised something of the importance of the relational substructure of the legal ordering of human affairs. Hohfeld's legacy—the "jural relation"—is arguably the beginning of wisdom on the matter.

7
Relationality Reconsidered

"Legal phenomena consist of unique psychic processes . . . expressed, incidentally, in the unique form of ascribing to different beings (not only to people, but to beings of various other classes, conceived of in the mind), or to certain classes of such beings, 'duties' and 'rights'; so that these beings, so conceived of, are seemingly found in certain peculiar conditions of being bound or of possessing special objects ('rights'), and the like." *Leon Petrażycki*[1]

The second and third Gordian Knots revisited

Hart's tendency (in a sense) to "apotheosise" legal rules as the pre-eminent legal concept, on the one hand, and his inclination towards "reductionism" of law-affected human behaviour to legal rules, on the other—as I argued in chapter 4—obscured the relational dimension of law-affected human behaviour and de-emphasised one of its most fundamental dynamics: social power. A theory of law might, perhaps, surmount this problem by perceiving law not solely as rules or norms (or giving undue emphasis to normativity in that sense), but as a *relational* medium that maintains power relationships among social actors and between those actors and state officials. In this chapter I wish to argue that it is possible to link key aspects of Hohfeld's analysis of "jural relations" with Weber's analysis of social power. In particular I will attempt to suggest ways in which the Hohfeldian jural relation—specifically, the right↔duty nexus—has an underlying social power dynamic. My aim is to provide a basis

---

[1] Leon Petrażycki, *Law and Morality* (Harvard University Press, Cambridge, Mass., 1955), 8. See also Jan Gorecki (ed.), *Sociology and Jurisprudence of Leon Petrażycki* (University of Illinois Press, 1975).

not only for addressing the Second and Third Gordian Knots, but to pursue a line of enquiry that is consciously interdisciplinary: demonstrating, in other words, how legal conceptual analysis of the Hohfeldian kind may inform an essentially sociological analysis of law as a site of social power. It is beyond the scope of this book, however, to attempt anything beyond an outline of the relevant field of enquiry.

The jural relation

In his analysis of the underlying social power dimension of legal relationships—for example, in his sociological concept of legal right—Weber laid the groundwork for, and demonstrated the relevance of, engaging in Hohfeldian-type legal conceptual analysis. Later in this chapter I will suggest that Hohfeldian jural relations may be regarded as relationships of social power in the sense that Weber contemplates. Tellingly, both Hohfeld and Weber accentuate correlativity: for instance, in the sense that the right of one may be regarded as the duty of another. In the legal world, social actors (and juridical entities such as corporations) are ideatively connected in a manner analogous to forms of social interaction or social relationships. Natural and juridical persons are, in other words, linked together in a legal nexus that echoes or replicates the social nexus.

Hohfeld, of course, did not analyse jural relations in terms of social power or by means of sociological concepts. Nor, indeed, was the conceptual apparatus of the jural relation entirely Hohfeld's invention. The expression "jural relation", appears to have originated in Hohfeld's juristic writings, however, and was later taken up by Albert Kocourek. While those writers were certainly the principal *twentieth century* "relational jurists" the essential idea of the jural relation probably had its historical origin at least as early as the Roman law concept of the legal bond (*juris vinculum*) which Justinian applied in the *Corpus Iuris Civilis*.[2] Yet, if Hohfeld was not the first to put forward the

---

[2] See *The Digest of Justinian* (University of Pennsylvania Press, Philadelphia, Pennsylvania, 1985), Vol. IV, D.44.7.3pr; *The Institutes of Justinian* (North-Holland Publishing Co., Amsterdam and Oxford, 1975), *Inst*. III. 13.pr.

notion of the jural relation, there can be little doubt that his configuration of jural relations represented one of the most original and enlightening contributions to the literature of analytical jurisprudence. Certainly, the outpouring of secondary Hohfeldian literature testifies to the influence which Hohfeld had in twentieth century legal theory.[3] But Hohfeld's lasting contribution to legal theory ironically does not lie in the fact that he articulated a *theory* of jural relations, although he unquestionably *theorised about* jural relations. Hohfeld would doubtless have been the first to deny that what he was attempting in *Fundamental Legal Conceptions*[4] was, in theoretical terms, anything more ambitious than a dissertation aimed at clarifying basic conceptions of the law. Indeed, for all its theoretical importance his dissertation often amounts to no more than an attempt to clarify various terminological usages prevalent in practical legal discourse.

Hohfeld's Scheme of Jural Relations

Hohfeld did not attempt to define "jural relation", reinforcing the view that his dissertation was essentially a practical one. Kocourek, on the other hand, whose approach was somehow more scientistic—though not necessarily more enlightening[5]—undertook a critical assessment of a number of possible definitions drawn mainly from the work of nineteenth century jurists. According to Kocourek, the jurist Puntschart recognised that Savigny had "vaguely apprehended" the *juris vinculum* element of the jural relation. Through the application of legal norms, legal bonds were created "by which persons were gyved to persons and persons to things for definite purposes within the purview of the law".[6] Puntschart had also shown how the

---

[3] Some of this literature is cited by Roscoe Pound in a footnote which is itself truly voluminous. See Roscoe Pound, *Jurisprudence* (West Publishing Co., St. Paul, Minnesota, 1959), Vol. IV, 83, n. 101.

[4] W N Hohfeld, *Fundamental Legal Conceptions as Applied in Judicial Reasoning* (Yale University Press, 4th Printing, 1966).

[5] See Albert Kocourek, *Jural Relations* (The Bobbs-Merrill Company, Indianapolis, 2nd ed. 1928). As Roscoe Pound comments: "But one cannot but feel that [Kocourek] . . . carries out schematic exposition and terminology far beyond what is practically worth while": above at n. 3, Vol. IV, 82.

[6] Albert Kocourek, above at n. 5, at 41–2.

"bond" idea runs through the whole system of Roman legal conceptions.

The Roman law notion of the *juris vinculum*, as we have seen, entered the writings of the Emperor Justinian, who applied it in his definition of obligation: "An obligation is a legal bond whereby we are constrained by the need to perform something according to the laws of our state".[7] The developed Roman law idea of a legal bond contained no other subjection than that of the duty to perform or pay damages. The language used by Justinian, however, had associations with bondage, and this more literal connotation reflected something of the true nature of obligation as conceived in early Roman law. It might be argued that it required only a step rather than a great intellectual leap to move from the notion of physical bonds or fetters to that of *conceptual* bonds. Here the conceptual linkage which gyved persons to persons and persons to things, to use Kocourek's phrase, was more important than the physical linkage.

The idea of jural relation as conceptual linkage finds its expression in Hohfeld's arrangement of relations in the form of a scheme of correlatives and opposites, in which jural correlatives represent each side of one jural relation, viewed from the respective points of view of each party to the relation.[8] Far from adhering to an exhaustively "imperativist" conception of law, as Hart misleadingly suggested, John Austin had anticipated this

[7] *The Institutes of Justinian*, above at n. 2, at 197: *Inst.* III. 13. pr. See also J A C Thomas' commentary at 198. Further, see *The Digest of Justinian*, above at n. 2, at 639: D.44.7.3.pr.; and W W Buckland, *A Textbook of Roman Law* (Cambridge University Press, Cambridge, 3rd ed. 1963), 406.

[8] Hohfeld, above at n. 4. Both "sides" of the jural relation may, for theoretical purposes, be conceived from the point of view of *Iudex*. But consider George W Goble's characterisation of the power↔liability relation: "All acts or omissions legally significant involve the exercise of powers. The word describes a relationship of two persons from the viewpoint of the dominant or controlling party. The same relationship is described from the viewpoint of the servient or controlled party by the term *liability*". (See "A Redefinition of Basic Legal Terms" (1935) 35 *Columbia Law Review*, 535, partly reprinted in Jerome Hall (ed.), *Readings in Jurisprudence* (The Bobbs-Merrill Company, Indianapolis, 1938), 516 *et seq*). See also Hans Kelsen, *Pure Theory of Law* (University of California Press, Berkeley and Los Angeles, 2nd ed., 1967), 166: "The reflex right is only the legal obligation, seen from the viewpoint of the individual toward whom the obligation has to be fulfilled".

correlativity when he defined legal right as "the creature of a positive law: and it answers to a relative duty imposed by that positive law, and incumbent on a person or persons other than the person or persons in whom the right resides".[9] An exaggerated "imperativist" portrayal—such as Hart's caricature of Austin—tends to view law purely in terms of the relationship between ruler and ruled: the command of a sovereign obeyed by a subject, or of a legislature obeyed by a citizen. It expends little effort in examining the relationship *between subjects* or *between citizens*. Austin was in no doubt concerning the relationality of law, and to that extent was quite "Hohfeldian": "[A]ll rights reside in persons, and are rights to acts or forbearances on the part of *other* persons. Considered as corresponding to duties, or as being rights to *acts* or *forbearances*, rights may be said to avail *against* persons".[10]

In *Fundamental Legal Conceptions*, Hohfeld arranges jural relations in *one* table organised around the dichotomy between jural opposition and jural correlativity. Subsequent writers have preferred to show jural correlativity and jural opposition (or jural "contradiction"[11]) subsisting together in *two* tables, one table relating to the right *stricto sensu* family of jural relations, and the other relating to the power family of jural relations.[12] The following tables are based loosely on those appearing in the eleventh edition of *Salmond on Jurisprudence*.[13] It should be noted that Glanville Williams, the editor, argued that Hohfeld's "privilege" was best conceived of as a "liberty (not)",[14] and Salmond himself preferred to substitute "subjection" for Hohfeld's "liability".[15] The two tables are arranged within

[9] From John Austin, *Lectures on Jurisprudence* (London, 3rd ed. 1869), reprinted in Jerome Hall (ed.), *Readings in Jurisprudence*, above at n. 8, at 442.

[10] Ibid., 450.

[11] See, generally, Glanville Williams, "The Concept of Legal Liberty", in Robert S Summers (ed.), *Essays in Legal Philosophy* (Basil Blackwell, Oxford, 1968), 121 *et seq.*, esp. 128 *et seq.*

[12] A distinction between rights "in the strictest and most proper sense" and rights "in a wider and laxer sense" is maintained in Glanville Williams (ed.), *Salmond on Jurisprudence* (Sweet and Maxwell Ltd., London, 11th ed. 1957), 269–70.

[13] Ibid.

[14] Ibid, 271–3. See also Glanville Williams, above at n. 11.

[15] *Salmond on Jurisprudence*, above at n. 12, at 270 and 275, n. (c).

rectangles, yet there is no necessary relationship between the rectangles for, as Salmond comments: "[T]he four concepts within each rectangle are intimately related to each other, whereas there is not the same relationship between the concepts in the one rectangle and the concepts in the other rectangle".[16]

In the tables, correlativity resides in *vertical* lines, while opposition or contradiction resides in *diagonal* lines.

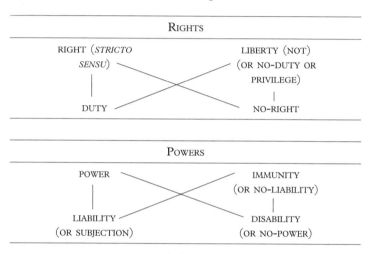

The derivative Hohfeldian arrangement shown in these tables is substantially in line with what has become a characteristically twentieth century theoretical position in which a principled distinction is drawn between, on the one hand, rights (and duties) and, on the other hand, powers (and "liabilities"). This distinction was, of course, brought to the forefront of more recent jurisprudential writing by Hart. Yet the Hohfeldian and Hartian analyses of legal powers do not coincide. Hart virtually ignores Hohfeld's analysis in *The Concept of Law*:[17] without doubt to the book's detriment. On a closer examination Hart's power-conferring rules are, on any ordinary language account certain-

---

[16] *Salmond on Jurisprudence*, above at n. 12, 270.
[17] H L A Hart, *The Concept of Law* (Clarendon Press, Oxford, 2nd ed. 1994).

ly power-conferring rules of a kind—but not of a rigorously Hohfeldian kind. Hart's distinction between power-conferring and duty-imposing rules centres upon perceived differences in the social functions which the respective rules perform. Although it is beyond the scope of this book to consider this further, there are very pronounced *analytical* differences between Hohfeldian legal rights *stricto sensu* and legal powers which Hart does not begin to address in *The Concept of Law*.

Jural Correlativity

Arguably, the key notion underlying Hohfeld's analysis—echoing sociological analyses of legal relationships in terms of social power—is that of *correlativity*. The notion of jural opposition (or contradiction) is also important to Hohfeld. He uses the expression "jural opposite" to denote a term which is the negative of another term. This yields two jural correlatives: the negative jural relation of no-right↔privilege (i.e., the jural opposite in the right *stricto sensu* family of relations) and the negative jural relation of disability↔immunity (i.e. the jural opposite in the power family of relations). But jural correlativity is perhaps a more fundamental concept. It underpins the relational nature of legal phenomena. The concept of jural opposition features only as a mode of classifying types of legal relationship.

In the eleventh edition of *Salmond on Jurisprudence*, Glanville Williams observes that the question whether rights and duties are necessarily correlative has resolved itself into two schools of thought according to one of which there can be no right without a corresponding duty, or duty without a corresponding right "any more than there can be a husband without a wife, or a father without a child".[18]

The other school of thought does not deny the correlativity of many rights or duties, or types of right or duty, but distinguishes between correlative rights or duties described as "relative", and rights and duties described as "absolute". Absolute rights in this sense have no duties corresponding to them, and absolute duties similarly have no rights corresponding to them. Neil MacCormick has argued that there are some rights—legal rights,

[18] *Salmond on Jurisprudence*, above at n. 12, at 264.

no less—which, being logically prior to any correlative duties, are therefore "dutiless" rights.[19] According to Williams, the dispute between the two schools is merely a "verbal controversy" devoid of practical consequences.[20] It may be that the dispute turns more upon how the words "right" or "duty" are used or defined in a particular context than upon the existence of any principled difference between relative rights (duties) and absolute rights (duties). The difficulty faced by the "absolutist" school, however—if the dispute is substantive rather than merely semantic—is to confront the underlying reality of norm-governed social action as "alter-oriented" behaviour. It is difficult, in other words, to visualise a right or duty that does not in some sense avail against some other person or is at least in existence because the world of human beings is a *social* world. This relationality, as we have seen, is reflected in the structure of social norms. Furthermore, the regulatory function of social norms—particularly *legal* norms, where the viewpoint of a legislator may be assumed—presupposes a situation where one person is required to act in a specified way, usually for the benefit of one or more others. Some of those "others" may indeed be in a position to enforce performance of the relevant requirement in a court of law.

It may be that arguments favouring a concept of absolute rights or duties turn less on the denial of the possibility that such rights and duties avail against "others", than on the determinacy (or indeterminacy) of the "others" against whom they avail. For instance, even if there is no one in particular against whom (say) Max might assert a right "to life", such an assertion would be meaningless were it not for the existence of "others"—multitudes of indeterminate "others"—who are, minimally, rational and intelligent beings more or less capable of understanding Max's assertion. The fact of making such an assertion involves at least a tacit assumption that those other beings have a "social nature". It may be the lack of determinacy of "others" against whom absolute rights or duties avail that lends support to the

<hr />

[19] Neil MacCormick, *Legal Right and Social Democracy* (Clarendon Press, Oxford, 1982), 161.

[20] *Salmond on Jurisprudenc*, above at n. 12, at 264.

"absolutist" school. It cannot be maintained, however, that lack of determinacy of such "others"—in the sense of difficulty of ascertainment of the specific individual or class against whom a right or duty avails—means *no one at all*. In the legal context the problem of identifying a party who "correlates with" the holder of an absolute legal right or bearer of an absolute legal duty may derive from a failure to visualise the right or duty in question in its "crystallised" form: that is, on the occurrence of relevant "operative facts". In such a case, an "uncrystallised" right or duty merely exists as an indeterminate hypothesis.

Correlativity also entails that the *content* of someone's right is precisely equivalent to the content of someone else's duty in terms of the subject matter of the prescribed act or forbearance. Similarly, in such a case, the content of someone's duty is precisely equivalent to the content of someone else's right. Mere contentual equivalence, however, does not entail that a right *is* a duty or a duty *is* a right.

If each term of a jural relation, whether it be right or duty, implies the other term—i.e., A's right implies B's duty and vice versa—it follows that in order to understand either term properly it is necessary to have regard to the correlative term. In the context of Hohfeldian jural relations each term is inherently relational in that the expression "a right" in some sense *contains* the notion of "a duty" owed by another party. An analysis that fails to convey the idea that a significant class of legal relationships—i.e., right↔duty relationships—entails the correlativity of a right that implies a duty and a duty that implies a right (corresponding respectively to the positions of superordinate and subordinate legal persons) is surely flawed or incomplete.

Legal relationships of social power

In his *Sociology of Law* Weber argues that social power (*Herrschaft*)—traditionally translated as "domination" or "legitimate authority"—is manifested in legal relationships. According to Weber, social power—the possibility of imposing one's will upon the behaviour of another person—emerges in a variety of forms. The rights which the law confers upon one person

157

relative to one or more others may be conceived as powers to "issue commands" to the other or others in question. Weber equates the "whole system of modern private law" to the "decentralisation of domination" in the hands of those to whom legal rights are accorded. Employees thus have power over their employers in the Weberian sense of "domination" to the extent of the employees' claim for wages.[21]

Weber stresses the distinction between "commands" directed by the judicial authority to an adjudged debtor and "commands" directed by the claimant to a debtor prior to judgment. An equivalent distinction exists between substantive legal relationships, such as those between litigating parties, and adjective legal relationships, such as those between court personnel—e.g., a judge—and litigating parties. A third class of legal relationships—which we might call *executory* legal relationships, such as those between enforcement organs and litigating parties pursuant to a court order—may be regarded as "commands" issued by the enforcement organ to the party identified by the court order. Such relationships, as I suggested in chapter 3, may be said to be governed by *rules of executive action*, commonly falling within the scope of administrative law. Thus, a version of the "Austinian" notion of "command" which Hart so decisively rejects in *The Concept of Law* is given a central role in Weber's characterisation of social power in the legal context. Legal relationships are conceived in terms of structures of "commands" not only at the level of—and as between—private individuals, but at the level of—and as between—the judicial authority (or enforcement agencies) and private individuals. The "commands" in question are, however, derivative: they result from the specific application of legal norms or rules in a given case. Kelsen, for instance, refers to this as "concretisation". For Kelsen, adjudication is simply a mode of norm production. A material fact determined in the abstract in a general legal norm requires to be established as actually existing in concrete cases. The judicial decision individualises the

---

[21] Max Weber, *Economy and Society. An Outline of Interpretive Sociology* (Bedminster Press Inc., New York, 1968) (*ES*), 942; Max Weber, *Max Weber on Law in Economy and Society* (Harvard University Press, Cambridge, Mass., 1954) (*LES*), 323–4.

general norm. Kelsen thus holds that the judicial function is constitutive in a unique sense:[22]

> "[I]t is law creation in the literal sense of the word. . . . Thus, the judicial decision is itself an individual legal norm, the individualisation or concretisation of the general or abstract legal norm. . . ."

Social Relationality and Correlativity

Examining more closely Weber's distinct concepts of social power, two separate but complementary standpoints emerge: one causal, the other "hermeneutic". On the one hand, Weber's concept of "domination" (or *Herrschaft*) and the wider concept of "power" (or *Macht)* emphasise the *de facto* or causal element of social power, expressed in terms of probability. For Weber, *Macht* is the probability that one actor within a social relationship will be in a position to carry out his or her will despite resistance, regardless of the basis on which this probability rests. *Herrschaft* is the probability that a command with a given specific content will be obeyed by a given group of persons:[23]

> "The concept of power is sociologically amorphous. All conceivable qualities of a person and all conceivable combinations of circumstances may put him in a position to impose his will in a given situation. The sociological concept of domination must hence be more precise and can only mean the probability that a *command* will be obeyed."

On the other hand, Weber offers a "hermeneutic" notion of power that lends weight to Alan Hunt's characterisation of power in the Weberian sense as a "relational concept", concerned as it is with the impact of one person upon another in so far as the behaviour of the one may be analysed as having been determined by the other.[24]

> "*Herrschaft* (domination) does not mean that a superior elementary force asserts itself in one way or another; it refers to a meaningful

---

[22] Hans Kelsen, *Introduction to the Problems of Legal Theory* (Clarendon Press, Oxford, 1992) *(PTL)*, 68.

[23] *ES*, 53.

[24] Alan Hunt, *The Sociological Movement in Law* (The MacMillan Press Ltd., 1978), 113.

interrelationship between those giving orders and those obeying, to the effect that the expectations toward which action is oriented on both sides can be reckoned upon . . .".[25]

Guenther Roth takes the notion of relationality one step further by characterising *Herrschaft* in the sociological sense as a "structure of superordination and subordination, of leaders and led, rulers and ruled".[26] This links in quite significantly to Hohfeld's analysis: superordination and subordination are mutually dependent and *correlative* notions. If A is superordinate to B, then B is subordinate to A; if B is subordinate to A then A is superordinate to B. In much the same way: if A has a right that B should φ, then B has a duty to φ relative to A. If B has a duty to φ relative to A, then A has a right that B should φ. Relationality and (a distinctly Hohfeldian) correlativity underlie both the Weberian concept of "domination" in the context of *legal* authority and the Weberian concept of legal right. In the legal setting "domination" equates to authoritarian power of command[27] involving a situation in which the will or command of a "ruler" is meant to influence the conduct of one or more others (the "ruled") and actually does influence it in such a way that the conduct of the ruled to a socially relevant degree occurs "as if the ruled had made the content of the command the maxim of their conduct for its very own sake". The conduct of the ruled is obediential. It is clear from Weber's further observations that the protean concept of domination extends beyond the context of "rule" in the sense of the rule of civil government, to more modestly scaled situations such as that of officials operating in different departments of a modern bureaucracy. Each official is subject to the others' powers of command in so far as the latter have jurisdiction. Such a "command structure" is present, according to Weber, even in the case where a customer places an order with a shoemaker for a pair of shoes.

Weber's sociological concept of legal right accentuates one aspect of the social power dimension of a right: the possibility of a "coercive apparatus" being invoked in favour of the right-

---

[25] *ES*, 1378. See also *ES*, 212–3.
[26] See Roth's footnote to *ES*, 61, n. 31.
[27] *LES*, 328.

holder's ideal or material interests. According to Weber, this aid consists in the readiness of certain persons to come to the right-holder's support in the event that the "apparatus" is approached in the proper way and that it is shown that recourse to such aid is actually guaranteed by a legal norm.[28] Weber's concept of (correlative) legal *duty* also emphasises relationality, whilst stressing that the legal relationship has an expectational element:[29]

> "The fact that a person 'owes' something to another can be translated, sociologically, into the following terms: a certain commitment (through promise, tort or other cause) of one person [B] to another [A]; the expectation [of A], based thereon, that in due course the former [B] will yield to the latter [A] his right of disposition over the goods concerned; the existence of a chance that this expectation will be fulfilled."

The social power element in Weber's sociological definition of a legal right perhaps lies more in the "readiness" of a "coercive apparatus" to be mobilised in favour of a right-holder's ideal or material interests, than in any quality that attaches to the right-holder personally. In emphasising the link between social power and the availability of an enforcing "coercive apparatus", Weber adopts the viewpoint of the *right-holder* rather than of the "apparatus". This is consistent with his contention that private law may be seen as the decentralisation of social power or "domination" in the hands of those to whom legal rights are accorded. The point was made in chapter 1 above that every right-holder is, in the first instance, potentially an enforcer of legal rights against relevant duty-bearers regardless of the actual or potential intervention of an organised "coercive apparatus". In seeking payment for goods or services a shop attendant does not normally rely on the imminent possibility of court intervention. Shop attendants—or, for that matter, bus conductors, taxi drivers, builders, car

[28] *ES*, 315; *LES*, 15–16.
[29] *ES*, 327. In this passage I have inserted references respectively to right-holder and duty-bearer ("A" and "B") in square brackets to clarify relationality in the situation described. Weber's concept of "legal relationship" designates "that situation in which the content of a right is constituted by a relationship, i.e., the actual or potential actions of concrete persons or of persons to be identified by concrete criteria". See *ES*, 319.

salesmen and others—are an initial point of enforcement of legal rights against duty-bearers. For their part, duty-bearers (e.g., "consumers") may accept without question that in a given situation they have a legal duty to offer payment for goods or services rendered to them. Hart makes an essentially similar point when he stresses that the function of law as a means of social control is best seen in the variety of ways in which law controls, guides and plans life *out* of court. On the other hand, it is essential to attend to the viewpoint of those who possess and exercise a more significant degree of social power relative to a particular legal right than the right-holders or duty-bearers themselves. Weber's sociological point of view urges the adoption of the perspective of those significantly invested with social power. The investigator's concern—indeed, the likely concern of the sociologically inclined jurist—is to discover what actually happens in a group owing to the probability that "those exerting a socially relevant amount of power" subjectively consider (legal) norms as valid and orient their conduct by reference to those norms.

A basic conceptual unit

Law is the embodiment of state power. It is both a manifestation and an instrument of social power which permeates every area of human activity. From a central site of origin, legal social power percolates to the nerve end of virtually every point of social contact between one human being and another. A first step towards understanding the nature of law as a site of social power is to perceive law not "as rules", but rather as a *relational* medium: one that creates power relationships among social actors, whether in the sense of private individuals, or others who perform a specific role, such as a judge or prison officer. Law creates relational structures of social power that may be examined both in the abstract and in specific contexts. It is possible to perceive those structures at a level of generality and abstraction that permits the discernment of an underlying universality of patterning. That patterning takes the form of legal relationships which, as I have argued, "translate" to Hohfeldian-type jural relations.

Given the apparent definitional interdependence of jural relational terms—the content of one person's duty being the content of someone else's right—it makes sense to regard the legal relationship as *one conceptual unit* and, following that through, as the basic unit of social thinking or sociological theorising about law. Just as for Talcott Parsons the structure of the relations between actors involved in interactive processes is "essentially the structure of the social system",[30] a legal system functioning as a "social system" is largely structured around the legal relationships between legal persons. The essentially social nature of legal phenomena is revealed in legal *relationships*, rather than legal norms, although structural elements of the legal norm facilitate a clearer understanding of that relationality. This is not to minimise the legal norm as a defining medium and as a linking medium. J W Harris notes that the concept of legal rule is logically prior to the concept of legal relation, and comments that "in all contexts descriptive information about the law may conveniently be given in terms of rules". He sees the legal relation as of use to legal science *only* in the context of litigation, which requires the position of opponents to be seen in relational terms.[31]

But whilst not denying that the legal norm is a "logically prior" unit, it is also arguable that relationality is so deeply embedded in the subjective meaning of *social* action that we cannot lightly ignore the manifestations of this in the legal context. The relationality of human social behaviour, as Hohfeld perhaps unwittingly taught us, *is* revealed in the concepts and conceptions ordinarily employed in legal thinking. Once recognised, it becomes clear that relationality in the legal context is merely a reflex of the more fundamental relationality of human behaviour in the wider social context. Inevitably, anything that is uniquely social and uniquely human will come to be manifested very markedly in the institutional and conceptual apparatuses of the law.

---

[30] Talcott Parsons, *The Social System* (The Free Press, 1951), 25.
[31] J W Harris, *Law and Legal Science* (Clarendon Press, Oxford, 1979), at 17.

8

Towards a Critical Legal Positivism

"In a way, they seemed to be conducting the case independently of me. Things were happening without me even intervening. My fate was being decided without anyone asking my opinion. From time to time I'd feel like interrupting everyone and saying, 'But all the same, who's the accused? It's important being the accused. And I've got something to say!' But when I thought about it, I didn't really have anything to say." *Albert Camus*[1]

Outline of a sociological perspective

I suggested in chapter 1 that the overarching rationale of this book was to develop the rudiments of a sociological perspective on state law and legal theory, drawing upon Weber's sociological and juristic writings. Weber's sociology was to be the context in which to explore themes developed from a critical reassessment of *The Concept of Law*.[2] The discussion in chapter 4 of three problematical areas, referred to as Gordian Knots—essentially a critique of key aspects of *The Concept of Law*—established a framework for a modified approach to theoretical enquiry into law briefly outlined in chapters 5, 6 and 7. In those chapters I sought to demonstrate how certain constructively modified elements of, first, Weberian sociology and, secondly, Hartian and Hohfeldian variants of analytical jurisprudence could be combined in a way that might facilitate the development of a distinctive theory offering an improved understanding of law as a social phenomenon. The type of theoretical enterprise suggested by, or

[1] Albert Camus, *The Outsider* (Penguin Twentieth Century Classics), 95–6.
[2] H L A Hart, *The Concept of Law* (Clarendon Press, Oxford, 2nd ed. 1994) (*CL*).

which has begun to emerge from, this approach is more Weberian than it is Hartian and is, in certain respects, more Hartian than it is Hohfeldian. It has been possible in this book to sketch only the beginnings of an outline of this interdisciplinary theoretical approach.

The emergent approach in the first instance stressed the importance of seeking to define the position of the jurist. A rudimentary role for the jurist—based on Weber's sociological point of view—would take as its starting point a more developed variant of the Hartian detached "non-extreme" external (or "hermeneutic") point of view, drawing upon debates centring on Weber's postulates of value-relevance (*Wertbeziehung*) and value-freedom: debates that still have currency in contemporary social theory. Following through the consequences of Weber's sociological viewpoint, the jurist might examine what "actually happens" owing to a "probability" that individuals—with the emphasis on those holding office in political or legal institutions—orient their social (official) action by reference to legal norms. The conceptual and analytical tasks suggested by that approach might then draw the jurist towards the extensive literature of analytical jurisprudence extending, but not limited, to Hohfeld's analysis and the work of, among others, the new analytical jurists identified by Robert Summers.

The further task of defining an institutional insider's point of view might lead the jurist to an examination of the role of the judge occupying judicial office at the hierarchically supreme level of a legal system. That might, but need not, result in the formulation of a Weberian ideal type, such as the *Iudexian* perspective, of which an outline was attempted in chapter 5. The construction of such a perspective would not rule out—or render less important—other perspectives: particularly of a "non-institutional" nature that could serve as a point of differentiation or contrast. For instance, let us say that authoritative ascriptions of institutional meaning—the "legal meaning" of human actions and legally significant events ascribed on the basis of conclusive findings of fact and authoritative interpretation of law—are conceived as emanating from a *Iudexian* standpoint: that of a hierarchically ultimate judge of an imaginary legal system sitting in the final court of appeal. This "ideal" supreme court judge may be used to present the realm of the legal as relatively autonomous and analytically separable, though not *empirically severable*, from the realm of the non-legal. An instance of human behaviour may appear quite different when seen respectively from an institutional viewpoint and a non-institutional viewpoint.

Another important task—outlined in chapter 6—was that of discerning the sense and extent to which legal norms have a role in structuring processes of social action or interaction. I considered a range of issues bearing on, or giving context to, that question including: first, the nature and structure of Weber's concept of social action and related concepts of social interaction and social relationship; secondly, the role of norms as part of the meaningful content of social action, social interaction and the social relationship, drawing, at appropriate points, on Hart's concept of "social rule"; and, thirdly, linkages between structural features of Weber's concept of social action and structural features of the social norm. The discussion of those and related issues led to the question of what it is that makes a norm governing human behaviour—more specifically, a duty-imposing (or right↔duty) norm—a "social" norm. I suggested that a norm may be described as "social" to the extent that it requires at least one party in specified circumstances to engage in a course of social action aimed at satisfying the expectations of at least one other party. I also suggested that the essentially social dynamic underlying behaviour governed by social norms is reflected: first, in structural features of social norms; secondly, in the relationality engendered by a norm governing social action where the norm constitutes a linking medium between social actors who apply the norm as a reference point for the orientation of their action; and, thirdly, in certain basic functions of social norms. I concluded that legal norms of the duty-imposing (or right↔duty) type by and large fit the analysis of social norms, and that many points of interface could thus be inferred between the social world and—so far as separable—the legal world.

I observed further in chapter 6 that at the level of private individuals much human behaviour, constituting social action in Weber's sense, can be regarded as being meaningfully oriented by reference to legal norms. Indeed, as Hart had noted, legal systems may owe their *existence* to this fact. Yet this failed to explain how it is that entire areas of human activity and other "facts"—even fictional events—can have legal consequences, whilst legal rights, duties and similar legal states can subsist often regardless of the state of mind of individuals most closely involved. In other words, those legal states can exist irrespective of whether the behaviour of individuals is meaningfully oriented by reference to legal norms and often regardless of the attitudes, beliefs, motivations or understanding—in short, the "mental content"—of those individuals. I suggested that the key to explaining this point of uniqueness is *institutionality*. I argued that the legal world possesses a unique property of institutionality based around the distinctive *institutional perspective* from which legally relevant behaviour and other factual events are perceived, and the *institutionally ascriptive* nature of legal phenomena. The nature of law as an institutionally ascriptive phenomenon, as I sought to demonstrate, resides primarily in the official activities of organised institutional structures: activities that constitute social action in Weber's sense. Those activities include adjudication. The theoretically conceived viewpoint of an "ultimate" judge, *Iudex*, discussed in chapter 5, could be regarded as the embodiment of a legal institutional (i.e., judicial) perspective. I argued that part of the judicial role is to engage in the conceptual act of ascribing evaluative meaning: (i) to the action of (among others) litigants or criminal suspects or other facts by reference to substantive norms; and (ii) to substantive norms in their application to the action of (among others) litigants or criminal suspects or other facts. This type of conceptual act includes that of perceiving the legal position of individuals in relational terms: that is, in terms of rights, duties and other legal relationships that may be loosely referred to as Hohfeldian-type relationships. The meaningful orientation of judicial social action by reference to legal norms—e.g., issuing a legally binding judgment—follows on the conceptual act of ascribing evaluative meaning. On the basis of such ascriptions of meaning—legal meaning—relevant "coercive apparatuses", invested with significant social power, are mobilised to take official enforcement action.

I further developed, and examined in closer detail, the notion of legal relationality in chapter 7, focusing in particular on key elements of the analytical work of W N Hohfeld. I argued that legal relationships (specifically, Hohfeldian "jural relations") may be analysed as relationships of social power. I concluded—without minimising the analytical importance of the legal norm—that the legal relationship might conceivably be regarded as the basic unit of social thinking or sociological theorising about law. I noted, finally, that relationality in the legal context is merely a reflex of the more fundamental relationality of human behaviour in the wider social context.

Towards a critical legal positivism

Is there an objective beyond sociological and juristic analysis that might be served by the approach outlined in the latter chapters of this book? The words of Meursault, the main character in the novel *The Outsider* by Albert Camus quoted at the beginning of this chapter, allow a glimpse of the mindset, and hence the paradox, of legal meaning. Often, the gulf between the "official world"—for example, an "official" legal interpretation of human behaviour or events—and the viewpoint of the private individual renders one point of view unrecognisable when juxtaposed against the other.

But the world view of a single individual may be relatively unimportant when weighed against perspectives that are representative of the existence of a *generalised* lack of consonance between those perspectives and institutional perspectives. For instance, frequently a class of individuals—or a specific group or community—holds a view or set of beliefs or occupies a situation whose "typical characteristics", so far as capable of ascertainment, are endemically similar. It may be possible in principle to apply those typifying characteristics as points of differentiation between the perspective of the relevant group and a perspective used as a benchmark such as an institutional viewpoint. The importance to theory of perspectives that are a counterpoint to an official, institutional perspective is more powerfully demonstrated when an *entire sector* of a community—e.g., an ethnic or minority group—is victimised by oppressive or discriminatory laws. Of course, there may be no necessary point of homogeneity or unifying principle that links one group or type of case with another. Inevitably, the circumstances of one group—e.g., exploited children in South Asia—may be so unique that they defy ready comparison with the circumstances of another group, e.g., the position of the indigenous majority in apartheid-era South Africa. "Non-institutional" viewpoints may thus be as diverse circumstantially as they are distinct geographically.

The analytical separation of law in the sense of state or institutional law—crudely, law "as it is"—from any standpoint from which law in this sense can be constructively and critically evaluated—law "as it ought to be"—is arguably itself a *moral imperative*. In *The Concept of Law* Hart acknowledges the need for clear-sightedness in recognising and confronting the official abuse of power. As Hart notes, it is necessary to "preserve the sense that the certification of something as legally valid is not conclusive of the question of obedience, and that, however great the aura of majesty or authority which the official system may have, its demands must in the end be submitted to a moral scrutiny".[3] A *Iudexian*-type or other institutional perspective may be a point of departure for the positivistic separation of expository and critical jurisprudence. It may be possible to develop such an enquiry towards a general critique of state law which, among other things, examines specific forms of legal repression, touching on the circumstances under which repressive legal structures arise and are maintained in existence. Typically recurrent structures of legal repression and legal dysfunctionality may be identifiable. Of necessity, however, the formulation by a sociologically inclined jurist of a perspective such as that of *Iudex* must immensely oversimplify the complex layering of beliefs, moral sentiments and motivational influences which inform the decision-making of a judge who, in acting in

---

[3] *CL,* 210. As Kelsen also observes: "[A]n absolute moral value is not called into question [by jurisprudence]. It may simply be that an absolute moral value goes unchallenged so that the merely relative value of the law might stand out all the more clearly against this background" (Hans Kelsen, *Introduction to the Problems of Legal Theory* (Clarendon Press, Oxford, 1992), 22).

the role of state official, might be seen in simplifying Weberian terms as an impersonal and mechanical executor of institutionally posited norms. As a human being, however (albeit idealised), *Iudex* is necessarily and ineliminably a moral agent implicated in all of the moral ambiguities, dilemmas of choice and conundrums of right and wrong afflicting any inhabitant of the human world. David Dyzenhaus comments on the dilemma of a judge in South Africa's Constitutional Court (Judge L W H Ackermann) compelled, by virtue of his official role, to apply morally repugnant apartheid laws:[4]

"As Ackermann tells us, he had been a judge of the Transvaal Provincial Division in 1980, but resigned to take up a Chair of Human Rights Law at the University of Stellenbosch in 1987. His resignation was prompted, he said, not only by his 'general ethical and jurisprudential' objections to apartheid, but also by his belief that 'the whole structure was irreconcilably at odds with my religious conviction that all humans are created equal in the image of god and indefeasibly equal in their fundamental dignity'."

I must hold over for discussion elsewhere the ways in which a "perspectival" approach to critical legal positivism—such as that briefly mentioned here—might be developed further. But at least it has been possible in this book to point in the broadest terms to the possibility of such an undertaking, whilst at the same time tentatively outlining a manifesto for the development of a modified—perhaps more explicitly sociological—approach to legal theory.

[4] David Dyzenhaus, *Judging the Judges, Judging Ourselves: Truth, Reconciliation and the Apartheid Legal Order* (Hart Publishing, Oxford, 1998), 78–9.

Index

Index

174

Index